SUCCESS

One Day at a Time

Collective

SUCCESS

One Day at a Time

Modus Vivendi Publishing Inc.

© 1998 Modus Vivendi Publishing Inc.

Published by:
Modus Vivendi Publishing Inc.
2565, Broadway, Suite 281
New-York, NY 10025

Cover design and illustrations: Marc Alain
Page layout: Modus Vivendi Publishing Inc.

ISBN 2-921556-57-X

Foreword

"He who lives for love spreads goodness and compassion all around him. He who ceases to believe in the virtues of the heart becomes a sterile soul, lost and wandering in the desert."
— FRANCIS HEGMEYER

*T*he I Ching, the Chinese Book of Changes, refers to the inferior being and the superior being. Inside each of us lies the possibility to choose between the high road or the low road. The individual can choose between a life based on the satisfaction of urges and personal interest or on the achievement of more noble goals.

When an individual listens to the call of his inferior characteristics, he gives in to the world of appearances, putting the physical ahead of the mental, living a superficial and finite existence. The inferior being knows nothing of virtue and is unable to achieve true success. The inferior being cannot come to know the deeper meaning of love and life. The inferior being is unable to see the dynamic forces inherent in life and events. The inferior being is doomed to fail because he has no access to profound knowledge or to the wisdom of the soul.

When an individual listens to the call of his superior characteristics, he reaches a new level of knowledge and self-awareness. He makes consistent use of his many sources of discernment, a faculty which springs solely from the spiritual. He looks at the world and sees far beyond appearances, he makes choices based on wiser and more valuable criteria and he directs his efforts and energy at reaching nobler goals. The superior being always triumphs because he values the virtues of the heart: gentleness, goodness and compassion. The superior being can achieve his goals with approval from the universe.

Virtue is the tool of choice for the superior being. The superior being is virtuous because he understands the strength and breadth of virtue. He knows that by being virtuous, he is true to his profound nature; he becomes the instrument of goodness and greatness. He knows that virtuous behavior brings him closer to the divinity within.

Introduction

*I*n preparing this publication, we set out to explore a subject that is extremely important in a world pondering values: the importance of ethics and the need for virtues. No one need look very far to see that it is impossible for an individual who fails to adopt a code of behavior rigorously founded on virtues and ethics to live in harmony with himself, to reach higher levels of personal growth or to succeed in the loftiest sense of the term.

In virtuous attitudes and behaviors, there is a superior logic, a path that leads directly to serenity, freedom and success. But along the way, we have forgotten or lost sight of the value inherent in all virtue. We have come to see goodness, gentleness, compassion and gallantry as old-fashioned and archaic, personality traits that have no place in the modern world. But virtues can never be outdated since they point the way to salvation, divinity and success. Virtuous attitudes and behaviors are identifiable manifestations of our true selves and they create an aura of dazzling light around us.

And so this publication is dedicated to virtuous action, because virtuous action carries within it the promise of success. Virtuous action inevitably leads us to success because it lays down a path from the heart to the material world of concrete accomplishment, from the subtle world of the soul to the tangible world of action and gestures. First and foremost, *Success — One Day at a Time* is a source of inspiration for all those who believe that noble action is the sure way to success because it is the ultimate manifestation of the human being's superior nature. *Success — One Day at a Time* can never be a substitute for an individual's self-awareness nor can it provide a sure recipe for life. However, it can serve to point the way for all those who seek to build and amass much, much more than mere comfort and material wealth.

The Dawn of a New Year

Now is the dawn of a new year
A new year stands before me
Like a mighty and beautiful oak

Now is a new opportunity
To do what I've always wanted to do
To become what I've always dreamed of becoming

Now is a new life
A life filled with love and pride

Now is the time to choose my way
As a being who has travelled far
To find a port, to weigh anchor

Now is the beginning of a wonderful adventure
Now I am ready to embrace the year ahead

Achieving My Objectives

I start this new day with the resolve to achieve my objectives. Today, I make a list of my most cherished objectives and I set deadlines for achieving them. As I draw up a list of my objectives, I consider not only my financial and material needs, but my emotional and spiritual objectives as well. I can build a life of quality. I know that I can achieve the objectives I have set for myself in all aspects of my life.

I am happy to be alive and to be able to look at my objectives and priorities. I know that as I do so, I am influencing my tomorrows. By setting my objectives for the years to come, I am consciously embarking on my journey into the future and I am totally responsible for what it will hold.

Standing on My Own Two Feet

I take pleasure in standing on my own two feet. I've always known that to be truly free and happy, I must be independent and self-reliant. At times I've been afraid and I've thought that I might not be able to meet my own needs, but now I know that no other person on earth can support and love me as much as I support and love myself.

I've always known that by working, I can protect my independence and my dignity. I don't wait for someone else to tell me what to do and how to do it. I am a competent and productive person. By working, I find self-fulfillment!

Allegiances

"In the Middle Ages, knights swore loyalty to their King, their Queen, their brotherhood... This was a time when one's word was priceless; a commitment involved honor and life itself and nothing nor no one could overturn an allegiance or a promise."

— ANONYMOUS

Our allegiances are the tangible and living proof of our commitment and our loyalty to our group and its ideals. We cannot succeed on our own. Living all alone with our material riches is like being a part of the living dead who wander the earth anonymously, unseen and unloved. To succeed, I must share my successes. I must abandon myself to a truth that is greater than me. Of course, each individual carries the spark of creation and energy within, but the group, the family, the parish, the party or the community leads to the accomplishment of major collective projects which can influence the future of an astounding number of people. And so my success as an individual depends on my belonging to a group and the allegiance I pledge to it.

Keeping My Word

"What we do today, at this precise moment, will have a cumulative effect on all of our tomorrows."

— ALEXANDRA STODDARD

Today, I understand the importance of honoring my commitments and keeping my word. Personal success can never be founded on cheating or lies. It must be founded on honor, dignity and trust. I know that I must trust myself and that I can rely on myself to do what I've said I would do. Keeping my word is a matter of self-respect and consistency.

Today, I respect my commitments and once I've given my word, I never go back on it. Keeping my word is a matter of honor. If I want to love and respect myself, I must be consistent and reliable. And above all, I want to live without guilt, knowing that I did all that I promised others I would do.

Down with Procrastination!

Today, I take action! All too often I waited and let too much time go by before I took care of certain problems or certain difficult situations. I must stop putting things off until tomorrow. Down with procrastination! From now on, I muster all the courage I have and I take action. I know that I am capable of living with the consequences of my choices and my actions.

Financial Independence

I work for my own independence. I see how our society encourages debts and dependence on financial institutions. Today, I resolve to pay back my debts. I borrow only if I know that I can pay back my debt promptly and I use my financial resources intelligently so that I can achieve financial independence.

Corruption

"Corruption can make people very rich. But those who use it should know that one day, they will be unable to find peace anywhere under the sun."

— François Garagnon

Of course, I work to earn a living. But I will never jeopardize my personal principles for the sake of financial gain. I am intelligent enough to recognize that crime and corruption sometimes look harmless and unthreatening from the outside. The consequences of small dishonest gestures aren't always clear and easy to see. But even though it's easy to commit small crimes without ever getting caught, each of us has to live with ourselves — and with our actions — for the rest of our lives. The human being can very easily perpetuate small dishonesties throughout a lifetime, justifying them with all kinds of faulty reasonings. But deep inside, he knows that he has committed a crime or a transgression.

Growth

Now, my aim is growth. I seek to achieve the best possible results and my ultimate target is perfection. I know that all things which fail to grow are doomed to eventual disappearance, so I seek to increase my productivity and to make my assets grow. By doing so, I feel stronger and more self-reliant.

Organizing My Work

Work calls for organization. The industrial revolution of the 19th century was based on the development of a new kind of work organization. Assembly lines, for example, revolutionized the production of durable and semi-durable goods. Today, with the development of computer technology, work is undergoing a new transformation. As a result, we have access to more efficient work organization. We are witnessing increased rationalization of production methods, aimed at increasing productivity and cutting production costs.

Today, I see that if I want to succeed, I must organize my work efficiently. By being systematic and coherent, by using the best work tools, I will be more productive and I will achieve better results. Any form of work calls for a form of organization designed to optimize results.

A Small Particle of Divinity

"Forgiving is looking at the person who has offended you in a totally different way: through the eyes of charity and love. It's a hard thing to do, but it can change a life because forgiveness breathes new life into a relationship and changes the chemistry between two people — from bitterness to tenderness."

— DAPHNE ROSE KINGMA

I have learned to forgive because in forgiveness, there is a small particle of the divine. Forgiveness is a sign of nobility. It is also a sign of greatness, because we must be capable of surmounting our bitterness, our anger and at times, even our pride if we want to choose the path of compassion. Forgiving is not something easy. But in difficult situations, once emotions are no longer at their peak, we must learn to forgive, if only to concentrate our attention and our efforts on something else. Anger is a very poor advisor and bitterness imprisons us in negativity.

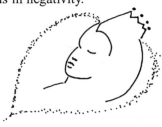

Succeeding One Day at a Time

I have decided that success is a life-long project that I must tackle one day at a time. I've decided that I must focus my efforts on day-to-day successes. Throughout my life, I have experienced some rather difficult times. I wasn't always absolutely sure that I would ever see better days. But now, I know what to do to be happy. I must work each and every day to achieve my goals. I must keep my eyes focused on my objectives and I must do the very best I can every single day. With this conscious and consistent approach to life, I know that I will find success.

A Gracious Heart

"Gracious acts reflect the soul that encourages them and lighten the body that carries them out."
— H. DESBOIS

Individuals whose hearts are gracious bring a touch of lightness and sweetness to everything in their surroundings. Grace is often associated with the arts. We use the word grace to describe a dancer, a sculpture or we say that the subject in a painting shows the artist's graceful touch. But grace is something we also find in a likeable and amiable person. Originally, the word meant "to witness kindness". Gracious is used to describe something given or done out of generosity: we witness gracious acts and donations are things graciously supplied to further a cause.

Grace is part of the extended family of virtues; it is the missing piece in the puzzle of life, the piece that makes the picture complete. Having a gracious heart or acting graciously means behaving in a kind and amiable way. It means opening one's mind and embracing the differences we see in others with tolerance and acceptance.

Tolerance enables me to work and mingle with everyone, while remaining respected and amiable.

The Light of Discernment

Discernment is the ability to judge things soundly and clearly. It is the tool our intelligence uses to distinguish right from wrong and true from false. When I consider the amount of information featured each day in newspapers and on television, I realize just how essential discernment really is. Without it, how can I make up my own mind on events and how can I avoid blindly believing everything I'm told? Discernment even shows me where to place my trust, who to associate with and which people to make my friends. In short, without the light of discernment, we are blind, even in the strongest light of day. And, we leave ourselves open to disappointment.

Sometimes I hear people talk about a sixth sense: instinct. "I had a good impression, a good feeling." I sincerely believe that we must listen more often to the messages that come to us from our inner selves. At times the sensation is vague, only a small doubt and we tend to say: "It's nothing. I'm jumping to conclusions." But if we take the time to dig a bit deeper, to listen more carefully, to ask a few questions, then we are likely to see that the conclusions we've drawn were right.

Being on Time

Being on time is one of the values I include in the way I choose to live. I know that being on time is extremely important for people who have been subjected to unpleasant surprises or in some instances, worse still, who have been rejected or abandoned. By being on time, I create a sense of security among those around me. By being on time, I'm telling them: "You are important to me, and so here I am, right on time!" Elaborate explanations are a very poor substitute to being on time. Punctuality is a virtue and if being somewhere or meeting someone at a prearranged time is truly impossible, I telephone in advance to make alternative arrangements or to warn the other person.

Action

Today, I choose action and in action, I find self-fulfillment. Action for action's sake is pointless. Instead, I seek to create a positive and lasting effect. I know that to take action, not only must I make a firm decision, I have to set a pace and persevere until I achieve my objective.

Competence

"It is not by doing things we like, but by liking the things we must do that we can discover life's blessings."

— JOHANN VON GOETHE

I define competence as the ability to carry out a task efficiently, to complete a project successfully and to achieve superior results. I consider the quality of competence to be a virtue, since it involves putting your heart and soul into what you do. Being competent is refusing to accept work that is done poorly or negligently. Regardless of what your work is — engineering, crafts, manufacturing — what you produce reflects your inner self.

Giving Myself Permission to Succeed

Today, I give myself full permission to succeed. I listen to myself, not to the negative messages that urge me to stop moving forward. I recognize that I will face many obstacles along the road to personal success, but I will overcome them.

Today, I give myself permission to succeed. I know that I have all the talent and intelligence I need. I choose to do the right things and to approach life with competence and determination today and every day.

A Winner's Attitude

Today, I develop a winner's attitude. By adopting a positive attitude focused on success, I can bring energy and determination to all of the projects I undertake. Winners want to win. Winners know that in the long run, with work and practice, they will win. Failure has no place in a winner's world. Winners may lose an occasional game, of course, but they use that opportunity to learn and to become wiser and even more skillful. Winners use all the lessons they learn to help them win even more.

Today, I adopt a winner's attitude. I now that I can come out on top and I know that eventually, my efforts will be rewarded. I look straight ahead and I walk confidently into the future. I use my inspiration and all my talent to succeed.

Where Are the Knights in Shining Armors?

*"If you help someone, someone will help you —
perhaps tomorrow, perhaps in a hundred years
from now, but someone will help you. Nature
always pays its debts... This is a mathematical
law and life is pure mathematics."*

— GURDJIEFF

Today, I see that I cannot succeed if I focus all of
my efforts and all of my energy on my personal
gratification. I must include others in the wonderful adventure called success. Because I am a
responsible person who gladly helps and supports
others, I rise above purely selfish preoccupations.
I am open to life and to others and I base my relationships on friendship and mutual help. Success
implies exchange and cooperation. And so, I am
prepared to help others and to include them in my
life.

Saving

"The poor seek riches and the rich seek heaven, but the wise man seeks tranquility."
— SWAMI RAMA

Saving — the art of managing financial resources by avoiding frivolous or needless expenses — is surely a virtue. It takes a great deal of wisdom to use the resources we have judiciously because the outside forces that encourage us to spend and to consume are very strong. It is important to understand that managing our financial affairs wisely enables us to reach a higher level of freedom.

When I refer to the virtue of saving, the furthest thing from my mind is greed or the tendency to penny-pinch. Instead, I think of all the great fortunes that were built on very little. The ability to find a golden opportunity may be an art, but refusing to waste is certainly a virtue.

Welcoming Obstacles

Generally, succeeding calls for a high level of determination and persistence. There are many obstacles on the road to personal success: high tax rates, government regulations, access to financing, the costs of training employees, fierce competition in the marketplace and economic cycles, to name only a few. But without obstacles the game wouldn't be worth playing. If we desire true success, not only should we accept obstacles, we should learn to welcome them. Obstacle provide stimulation and real challenge.

Today, I see that success is based on self-affirmation. I am convinced that I deserve to take my rightful place among the architects of our society. I welcome the obstacles I find along my road and I look forward to the challenge of overcoming them.

A Positive Attitude Towards Life

Today, I know that a positive attitude towards life is crucial to success. I begin each of my projects with the intention of succeeding. Each day, I take on life with the feeling that I can seize every opportunity I encounter and I can make the most of every experience. Even when I fail at something, I try to see the positive aspect. I can change even my most difficult experiences into victories. I believe that without this positive attitude, I would often feel helpless and alone because life can be hurtful and brutal at times.

My positive attitude is my shield. It protects me against feelings of disappointment and depression. By taking a positive attitude towards life, I always feel that ultimately, things will work out fine. When I go to bed at night, I am confident that tomorrow will be a better day. My positive attitude acts like wings that lift me and carry me forward. I am capable of finding courage within me, of consoling myself and of giving myself the inspiration I need to nurture a positive attitude towards life.

The Indulgence of Power

"The quality of indulgence cannot be faked; it falls on our heads like a gentle rain from heaven; its blessing is twofold; it blesses he who gives it and he who receives it."
— WILLIAM SHAKESPEARE

How far does my responsibility extend in today's world? I readily admit that I am responsible for myself. It is also clear to me that I am responsible for my children and my immediate family. If I am a team leader, foreperson or supervisor, I know that I am responsible for my sector and my employees. But does my responsibility extend farther? I may have the impression that I cannot be responsible for areas that are beyond my direct control. But what I realize is that as I increase the scope of my responsibilities, I reach a higher level of consciousness and power. And as I take on greater responsibility, I must show a greater degree of indulgence towards others.

Honoré de Balzac said: "All power is a composite of patience and time. The powerful intend and attend."

Reaching Critical Mass

When a company or a project reaches critical mass, it is very hard to stop the process. In the early stages, when the foundations of the company or the project haven't been completely laid, it is much easier to stop things from developing.

So to succeed in every undertaking, it is important to reach critical mass, a certain weight, a certain speed. This is the best guarantee of survival and growth. Once critical mass has been reached, our velocity and our size make it possible to ensure our continued existence. And so it is important to reach critical mass quickly in all projects we want to make a success.

Looking Without Thinking

In our societies influenced by trends in scientific thinking, we tend to attach great importance to the act of thinking. But there is a different and very effective way of understanding reality: seeing. Our success depends on our ability to see. By seeing things as they are and by seeing how things change and grow, we can detect the real momentum and trends in the world around us. I resolve to make my vision sharper and not to depend too much on thinking.

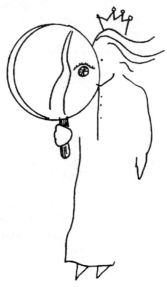

Small Victories

Today, I am aware that at times I must find my satisfaction in small day-to-day victories: a good meeting, a satisfied customer, a delivery made on time, a job completed. Success is filled with small daily victories and numerous gestures and accomplishments. Individuals who want to succeed have to know how to nurture these small victories if they want to cross the desert and find the way to the promised land. Today, I see small victories as pearls found along the road to making my dreams come true. These small victories nurture me and quench my thirst.

Today, I see that most important projects take time to finish. A company rarely reaches maturity before several years go by. So today, I take note of small victories. All these little things that tell me I am actually moving forward and drawing closer to my goals.

Living and Growing with Simplicity

Is it complicated to look at life simply? In the evening, after dinner, why not go for a brief stroll instead of sitting through all the bad news that the television brings into our living rooms. In the morning, before rushing into the day's traffic jam, I take a good, deep breath. I spend a few seconds contemplating the scenery around me. I look at the trees, the clouds; I listen to the birds singing; in short, I open my eyes and my heart to the simple things that Nature offers. In a matter of moments, I rid my mind of all problems, real and imagined.

Today, on the road to success, I take the time to breathe. I resolve to develop an inner calm by looking around me and taking pleasure in life — simply. I know that it can be hard to truly enjoy life when time is short and there are more than enough things to do. So I take the time to live and grow — simply.

People Who Block Our Ascent

There are people who sincerely want to help and contribute to our ascent. Some people are preoccupied with their own business and fairly indifferent to our victories and our defeats. At first glance, still others seem willing to help us, but in the final analysis they demolish and sabotage our accomplishments. I can live with the first two types of individuals, but I refuse to live with the third. Over the years, I have developed the ability to identify the saboteurs of success more rapidly. They can be charming or reserved, brilliant or stupid, flamboyant or withdrawn. Nevertheless, there are a number of clues that help identify them: they don't keep their word; they never finish their projects; they ruin the flow of communication; they cause errors, spread confusion and are always ready to point the finger at someone else.

Today, I look around me and I identify the people who block my ascent. I look for clues that indicate that person as someone who creates chaos, confusion and conflict in his or her immediate surroundings. I react quickly to rid my life of these saboteurs.

Being an Active Member of the Community

I look around me and I see that the world I live in needs me. I see hardship, conflict and despair taking over our cities and our communities. Today, I decide to be an active member of my community and to make a contribution to the well-being of those who share my life. I see that there are many, many things I can do to improve the quality of life in my neighborhood: I can encourage recycling, get involved in meetings held by the local business association, donate items and time to organizations who help families in difficulty and set up a neighborhood watch program.

Today, I see that my success depends on the quality of life in my community. I am a full-fledged member of this community and I want to make it a better place to live in. My ideas and my abilities as a leader or an organizer can help solve the problems facing the people who share my community.

Success and Spirituality

Those who believe that success is accumulating material wealth, belonging to the best clubs and sending their children to private schools are wrong about the fundamental nature of success. There is nothing wrong with material comfort, but it is only one aspect of success. The spiritual life of individuals plays a crucial role in the quality of their lives and experiences. It should never go ignored. And each of us is free to find a special way to express our spirituality. For some, spirituality is a sense of belonging and a willingness to participate in a religion. For others, spiritual life is expressed in their acts of kindness towards others and in the respect of a moral code based on justice and compassion. For others still, spirituality is expressed in the development of a higher level of consciousness through prayer and meditation.

Human being must recognize that first and foremost, they are spiritual beings and there exists another world, far beyond physical appearances.

A New Day

Today, I greet this new day, a day filled with hope and possibilities. I open my eyes to the dawn of a new life, a new beginning. Today, I give myself all the inspiration and all the confidence I need to succeed. I want to grow and to take my rightful place in this world. I want to be proud of my contribution to my love relationship, to my family, to my community and to my society. I want to act responsibly and creatively and I want to build a better world. I know that I can make a difference. I know that I can bring joy and love to my work. Today, I greet life. Today, I greet myself. I greet the wonderful person I am.

Doing One Thing at a Time

I have realized that doing one thing at a time is better than getting involved in several activities at the same time. Yes, I have many interests and variety is the spice of life. But I have to make sure that I finish each of the projects I decide to undertake and to do so, I have to give my all and I have to give it to one thing at a time. When I'm tempted to do several things at once, I spread myself too thin and I lose track of what I'm doing.

Today, I resolve to give up the idea that I can do everything at once. I focus my attention on one thing at a time and I finish what I've started. At the beginning of the day, I make a list of the important things I have to do today and I set priorities. Then I do one thing at a time, from start to finish, and then I move on to the next activity.

The Secret to Success

When I realized that I was completely responsible for my fate in life, I stopped believing in magical solutions and miracle recipes for success. Success is a dish made with a certain number of basic ingredients:

— a deep and unshakeable desire to achieve an objective that we have already identified;

— systematic and ongoing work to achieve the objective, no matter what factors and obstacles may appear to block my way as I try to reach my goal;

— the ability to recognize and celebrate the achievement of an objective.

Of course, there are predetermined factors that can help or hinder me in the achievement of my objectives. But these factors are completely incidental when the objective is clearly identified and when we resolve to do all that we can to achieve it.

Building Reserves

Our parents and grandparents understood how important it was to save. They have lived through very difficult times when it was often hard to find food and clothing. Their generation was profoundly affected by the hardship and poverty of the Depression. Today, society encourages us to consume today and pay tomorrow. And in the process of accumulating material wealth and amassing personal debts, at times we forget how important it is to save and to build a reserve fund.

Today, I realize how important it is to build financial security. The gesture of setting a certain amount aside each week or each month proves that I am ready for every possible event. I can be self-reliant no matter what happens.

My Inner Wisdom

With time, I've learned that I must focus on my inner wisdom. I have realized the greatest of all truths is what I learn through those who share my life, through my own personal experiences, through my own senses and through my own wisdom. There is no truth more vital or more precious than the wisdom I can find within me. I know that I must always listen to myself, my feelings and my perceptions. When I do, I will succeed in being loyal — to myself and to my principles.

When I begin a project, I decide to trust my inner wisdom. I focus on my feelings and my percep- tions. I let them guide me because I know that my perceptions will lead me to the right decisions and to the ultimate achievement of my goals.

Being Indispensable

There is a very basic truth that workers in today's business world often fail to understand: a resource is valuable only if it cannot be replaced. This is equally true of material and human resources. If a business or organization can replace a resource while saving money and keeping service at the same level, it will. Ideologies, sentimentality, the personality cult, unions, and government rules can only delay the process.

Today, I know that I have to make myself indispensable. By working intelligently and honestly, I have to offer the best quality of service to my employer, to my clients and to my colleagues in the workplace.

The Power of My Dreams

Today, I let myself dream and I resolve to make my dreams come true. When I was much younger, I had all sorts of projects and all sorts of goals in mind. I imagined my life and my future and I was nurtured by my dreams. It seemed that I could see myself growing and achieving my goals. The ability to dream let me build and choose; and more importantly, it let me rise above the problems and dullness of day-to-day life. But gradually, my dreams faded away and I lost my ability to dream. Now I know that from the time I stopped dreaming, I stopped living creative experiences.

Today, I nurture my dreams because I know that in them, I can find the seeds of my future successes. Today, I let my imagination run free and I see my ideal future played out before my eyes. The ability to create dreams gives me hope and inspires me in my day-to-day life. Today, I dream and I resolve to make my dreams come true.

Self-Confidence

"Some men achieve success because they are firmly convinced that their lives could never be otherwise. Success gives them total fulfillment. Not even the smallest of gaps can let failure filter into their lives. This certainty is a lot like auto-suggestion. In all circumstances, everything unfolds as if failure cannot possibly affect them, as if they are immunized against any kind of negative germ."

— FRANÇOIS GARAGNON

Succeeding, achieving my objectives and making my dreams come true call for certainty. The certainty that I can find the means and the inner strength to reach my goals. In the final analysis, in the battle of life, I must be able to rely on myself. I have to maintain the energy I find in new beginnings and I have to find a path that leads me to my ultimate goal. No one can give me self-confidence, not even the encouragement of my friends and my loved ones. A mental outlook that excludes the possibility that I might fail or that I might give up is my best asset. I have to believe in myself and I have to know that I will reach my objective no matter what life brings me. My resolve is to believe in myself and to trust the inner wisdom that tells me that I can reach my ultimate objective.

Making Failures a Positive Experience

"Most of the limits in our lives are those we impose on ourselves. Whenever we are firmly convinced that we can achieve something, generally we do. But conviction is something very different from wishful thinking. Taking your wishes for reality is a passive tactic; conviction and self-affirmation makes us clear a path through life's obstacles or maneuver around them to reach our ultimate goal."

— SUE PATTON THOELE

I have to assess myself against an objective reality. I have to look at the consequences of my actions and learn from them. Failure is the environment's objective reaction to what I do. When I fail, I have to determine exactly what actions, what behaviors or what factors have contributed to my failure. Failure can teach me a lot. In life, we learn much more from our failures than we ever do from our successes.

Today, I realize that life will always have something new to teach me. I will use my failures to learn and grow stronger. I can embrace failure instead of trying to run away from it by refusing to take risks.

Work is Noble

"Generally speaking, security is only a superstition. It does not exist in Nature and most human beings never truly experience it. Over the long term, avoiding danger whenever you can is every bit as unhealthy as exposing yourself to danger whenever you can. Life is either a thrilling adventure, or nothing at all."

— HELEN KELLER

Work is a source of freedom and self-determination for individuals and society as a whole. When I work, I am useful and I take up my rightful place in society. When I work hard, I become indispensable. When I am productive, I achieve self-fulfillment. To be truly free and happy, every individual must be self-reliant and independent. When I work, I can stand on my own two feet. When I am productive and competent, I earn the respect and admiration of others. When I work honestly, I can achieve all my objectives.

I Am a Business

I have learned to see myself as if I were a company. A company has a mission, objectives, resources and a workforce. I now that I must invest in my own professional development. I must define my mission and my objectives. I must acquire and maintain productive resources. I must seek to increase the efficiency of my workforce. In some ways, I am the president of my own company and I must behave like a good manager, not a greedy entrepreneur.

My work is my most precious resource. It nurtures my development and lets me build the future I want. I no longer wait for others to offer me things. I make a plan and I take action.

Real Obstacles

For a long time I thought that life was a battle and that in my environment, there were major obstacles to my success and to my happiness. I thought that life was the same for everyone and that the only option I had was to use all of my intelligence and all of my resources to overcome adversity. But gradually, I realized that the obstacles to my success were of my own making and that I couldn't hold others responsible for them.

I know that I can overcome the obstacles that I encounter. I can find a way. I can find a solution to every problem and every hard situation. But when I believe that I am unable to finish a project or when I am afraid to start a new one, the obstacles I have created for myself are impossible to overcome.

Today, I see that the obstacles that keep me from achieving success come from within. My first step is to eliminate any doubt, worry or apprehension that I am harboring. When I choose to knock down barriers that I have created myself, I can reach all of my goals.

Avoiding Panic

On my road to success, I will encounter a number of different situations. At times, situations may be urgent or dangerous. I have to keep calm and I have to resist the urge to react in panic or in anger. Most problems can be solved with good communication and small adjustments to behavior patterns. But when I react too strongly to a situation, I run the risk of not finding a solution to it. And in any event, if I react negatively, my reaction will have a negative effect on my colleagues.

Today, when I am faced with a problem or a difficult situation, I keep calm. I communicate with the people involved in the situation and I work with them to find a solution that will move things forward. I am not afraid to make changes and to find solutions to the problems that I can encounter on my road to success.

Difficult Relationships

I have realized that I cannot move forward and succeed unless I have the support of others. A crucial ingredient in mutual help and cooperation is the respect we show to others. In general, people are very sensitive and they react badly to anger, power games or punishment. When I realize that I have to show anger to get results, I know that I have a problem on my hands. Hard situations call for mutual help and cooperation, not anger.

At times, some of the people who share our work lives refuse to show any spirit of cooperation. Instead, unconsciously, they seek to stop us from achieving our goals. The best solution in such cases is to put a quick end to nonproductive and negative relationships.

Today, I realize that my relationships should be based on mutual help and cooperation. When a relationship involves conflict, frustration and anger, I must react quickly to change it in any way I can.

My Skills

"If you nurture the seeds within you, they will lead you to salvation. If you fail to nurture the seeds within you, what you fail to nurture will ultimately destroy you."

— JESUS CHRIST

Each person has individual skills, qualities and aptitudes and each person uses them to reach self-fulfillment. When I look for a job or when I want to start a new career or a new business, the most important question I must ask myself is: How can I use my particular skills to do work that I enjoy? There is a relationship between my aptitudes, my talents, my strengths and the kind of work that is best suited to me. Too often, people choose a job or a career based on criteria that are not really important: prestige, what family members expect, salaries, location.

I have my own special qualities. I must accept the challenge of developing my abilities and my talents regardless of preconceived ideas and any other factors. I must be true to my inner self and to my skills.

Refusing to Be Afraid

"Taking action despite fear is a proof of courage. Surprisingly, we act this way almost every day. If we were unable to face our fears, which of us would ever have changed jobs or moved to another city? Furthermore, which of us would tackle the constant need to arrive at a better understanding of ourselves if we were devoid of courage?"

— SUE PATTON THOELE

I know that I must confront my fears every single day. When I confront them, they seem so much smaller. Anxiety and uncertainty are totally normal reactions to the unknown and to hard situations. Therefore, I resolve to use all the inner courage I have and to face every situation I encounter. When I face my fears, I can grow and I can move closer to self-fulfillment. The road to inner harmony is filled with stumbling blocks. But I know that no obstacle and no fear is big enough to stop me.

Controlling Time

"Go slowly, breathe deeply and smile."
— THICH NHAT HANH

I can have a determinant influence on time. I have realized that I used to let time control my life. Time determined where I went and what I did. Time determined my quality of life. I had let a simple measurement system take control of my life experience. I could see time's effect on me, on my body and on my experiences and I felt that I could do nothing to change things. In a way, I thought I had to suffer the effects of time, that I had to fight as hard as I could against its negative effects.

I have stopped letting time control me and force me to rush forward blindly. I refuse to let myself be swept away on incessant waves of activity and I refuse to let my attention be drawn from the present moment. I have realized that I can control time. I can change how I see time. I can free myself from a negative perception of time.

I Am a Cautious Swimmer

"When you're caught in a ground swell that sweeps you out to sea, there's no use fighting and trying to swim to shore. You have to let go, you have to stop going against the current. When you let go, you let the current carry you gently and you can navigate your course and get to shore much more easily."

— A CAUTIOUS SWIMMER

I have realized that applying direct force is rarely useful. Things and individuals seek equilibrium. What is in movement seeks to remain in movement. What is stationary seeks to remain stationary. When I confront something with force or violence, I sometimes fail to take into account the nature and characteristics of that something. It is preferable to observe and to adjust to the situation at hand rather than apply force immediately.

Of course, I can't let events carry me away like a leaf on running water. But by recognizing the nature and cause of a situation, I can develop an approach that is appropriate and positive. I must also recognize the power of my decisions, which can also have a determinant influence.

My Natural Skills

I have natural skills, things that I do well, almost naturally. When I undertake an activity that I understand fully, I feel completely comfortable. As a result, I am in harmony with my inner self and with my environment. I feel competent when I undertake an activity that matches my natural skills. When I find a way to express my natural skills, I feel good and I feel in control.

Today, I will make a list of my natural talents and skills. When my list is done, I will look at how I can include my natural talents into my day-to-day activities. If I see that I am leaving one of my talents unused, I will look for ways to include that talent in my life and I will resolve to use it as often as I can.

My Worries

"We must plan for the future, but we need not worry about it. Planning is reassuring, worrying is a needless disturbance. Planning makes you stronger, worrying makes you a victim."
— SUE PATTON THOELE

Worrying is a vague and general feeling of fear, with no specific focus. Worrying is the result of fear of the unknown and a preoccupation with what could happen tomorrow. The only thing I can be sure of is that I am here right now. I have had to face difficult situations and I have overcome them. I will have to face challenges in the future and I know that I have all the capacity and all the resources I need to handle them. When I begin to worry, I tell myself that worrying is useless. I resolve to deal with the here and now and I refuse to try to predict future disasters.

Each Moment is New

"As long as there's life, there's hope."
— JOHN LENNON

Today, I know that each minute brings me new possibilities and a new window I can choose to look through. Each minute is a new opportunity for me to change. Each day is a chance to reinvent myself. I can look at situations differently. I can enjoy every second in a day and I can see that my life is a process of constant change.

Today, I see that my success is based on my capacity to adapt and to change. I no longer cling to situations I have experienced in the past. I look at and analyze the present situation and I use what I see in it to grow. Each day is completely new and filled with new experiences, each minute in the day brings with it new possibilities, and each breath I take brings new hope into my life.

Succeeding

Success is something that can be defined in many different ways. I can succeed from the material or financial point of view. I can succeed on the emotional level by creating a stable and happy family. I can succeed professionally by building an interesting career. I can succeed spiritually by reaching higher levels of consciousness and by achieving wisdom and serenity. Success is satisfying. Success makes me believe in my abilities and my determination. Success is noble as long as I reach it without hurting anyone else.

Succeeding means making the goals I imagine for myself goals that I can actually achieve. It means making my dreams come true. It means taking on the challenge of setting things in motion and making sure that they go in the direction I want. Today, I focus on success. I look at my life and I see all of my successes. I look at how I achieved them and I use the same strategy in all aspects of my life.

Contributing to the Success of Others

How can anyone succeed without contributing to the success of others? The answer is: it's impossible. Today, I can see that my success is narrowly linked to the success of others. I have surrounded myself with people who love me and who want to contribute to my success. In the same way, I am responsible for their success and I am very happy to embrace that responsibility.

Today, I know that I must contribute to the success and happiness of others if I want to succeed. Such are the laws of the universe. I can't hope to succeed if the people around me are experiencing hardship or uncertainty. So I contribute to the success of the people who share my life and I help them achieve their objectives whenever I can.

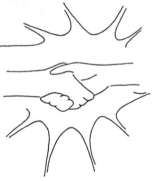

My Destiny

I realize that my life is exactly the way I want it to be. My life is not the result of a series of coincidences or accidents, it is a series of choices I have made for myself. My life is not something my parents, my partner or my children have planned for me. The quality and type of life I live is not the result of my education or my genetic background. My life was built by me, choice by choice, gesture by gesture. I am an aware, responsible and energetic being. Ultimately, I am responsible for my own fate.

Today, I embrace all the responsibility and all the joy that comes with the realization that I am the person who is responsible for my own destiny. I am in control of my choices, of my actions and of my life.

We Never Stop Learning

The beauty of life is that we never stop learning. Life always has new lessons in store for us. When we are open to learning new things, life is full and life becomes a wonderful adventure. When we are open, we see everything under a new light, we improve our skills and our capabilities, we achieve better results in our work lives and we make our relationships better.

Adapting, learning and success are all closely linked. When I can learn and adopt new approaches, I can succeed. When I am closed, life is closed to me and I experience more and more difficulties.

Today, I am open to learning. I know that my success depends on my ability to learn and to adapt. When I embrace all of the lessons life can teach me, I feel alive and open.

I Am My Own Guru

Have you ever noticed that there are experts, consultants and gurus on just about every street corner? Today's society produces an amazing number of experts who are ready to show us how to live, how to manage our lives and our businesses, and how to solve our problems. Based on their advice, we should find the sure path to happiness and prosperity!

I have decided to be my own guru. My inspiration is based on my own experiences, my own knowledge and my own ability to observe and learn. I am open to the viewpoints of others and sometimes, I can even use them as an inspiration. But I know that I am the only person who can live my life and who can shoulder the consequences of my decisions. Ultimately, I am responsible for my own fate and I must live with my own successes and failures. So now, I save time and money: I consult as few gurus as possible!

Today, I resolve to take my own advice. Today, I will base my life and my gestures on my own inner knowledge. Today, I resolve to give up the notion that I have to depend on outside advice to succeed. I am open to new ideas, but I am the person who makes the final decision!

Finding the Right Recipe

With time, I've come up with my own recipe. It's easy and I want to share it with you.

1) I work in a business that I love and that makes the best use of my talents.
2) I strive to give the best possible service and the best quality products to my clients and I constantly look for ways to improve my service and my products by adapting them to specific needs.
3) I maintain a consistent work pace and work quality and when I need to pick up my work pace, I delegate.
4) I surround myself with people, clients and suppliers who share my commitment to quality and who are people I like working with.
5) I pay all of my invoices on time and I ask that my clients do likewise.

Each person can come up with his or her own recipe. Today, I realize that my recipe must let all those who are affected by my business activities feel positive and successful.

Debts

Society gives us access to a number of different sources of credit which can offer a number of advantages. But the advantages of credit disappear very quickly when our income drops. Debt is one of the most effective type of social control, even though it isn't necessarily all negative. When it is well managed, credit can provide flexibility and it can open up new roads to help us achieve our goals.

Money borrowed to get an education, to build up a business or to make an investment to generate additional income doesn't have the same effect on our lives as money borrowed simply to buy more things. Borrowing money to maintain a lifestyle or to create the appearance of material wealth is always much, much too expensive.

Today, I manage my credit wisely. I agree with the idea that to buy more things, I have to earn more. I use my credit to build up my business or to get an education. I always pay my debts and I borrow only if I know that I can pay back the amount I've borrowed.

Travelling Through the Desert

Yes, I have experienced the cold of the Far North,
But my best memories are the vast expanses of
the land.

Yes, I have crossed the desert,
But my best memories are the sunsets I saw.

Yes, I heard the blast of bombs in my war-torn
country,
But my best memories are the friendships I made.

Yes, I have experienced personal failure,
But my best memories are moving on to new successes.

Highs and Lows

Anyone starting a new business can expect highs and lows. After the first burst of energy that any new beginning brings, there is a much longer period of stabilization that involves getting a product known, establishing a work structure, and creating a team of reliable contributors and suppliers. The process takes time and a great deal of energy. And the outset of this kind of adventure brings all sorts of new situations that serve to test our good judgement and our commitment.

But when the groundwork is done, it becomes easier to see long-term stability and to enjoy the rewards of work well done. Today, I know that beginnings are always hard. I am more vigilant at the outset and I use my judgement to choose reliable team members who share my values.

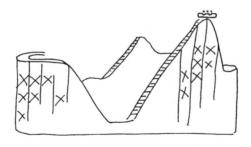

Writing Thank-You Letters

Today, I will take the time to write thank-you letters to the people who have contributed to my success. And I'll write them by hand to make my communication even more personal. From now on, I will take the time to write thank-you letters to express my appreciation. By writing thank-you letters, I can reinforce the relationships that are important to me and I can encourage the people who work closely with me.

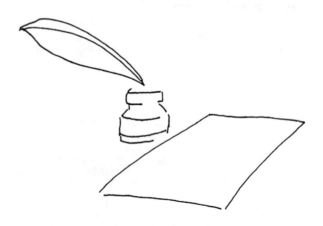

The Question of Ethics

Today, I look very closely at the people and organizations that I do business with. At times I have been trapped into unfortunate situations, with people who had no moral or professional ethics. Our society is filled with people who believe that they are smarter than anyone else. They are convinced that they can pay their bills late, fake their accounting records and deliver inferior quality products and services. Even if these individuals and the businesses they manage are doomed for extinction, they can have a very negative effect on the people who happen to cross their paths.

So I am vigilant and I look for signs: appealing lies, repeatedly and increasingly late payments, shoddy work and endless lists of reasons why deadlines have been missed. Today, I surround myself with people who share my values of integrity and honesty in the business world and in everyday life.

Looking for Competence

Business people often say that it's hard to find a good, competent employee. Despite the phenomenon, unemployment offices and employment agencies are filled with people who say that they would do anything to find a good job. The gap between the two perceptions is considerable. The deterioration in the quality of work provided by employees has led today's businesses to build a very small nucleus of competent and hardworking people and to delegate a variety of tasks to outside workers.

In our society, competency is a quality that is increasingly valuable, so if I want to sell my work, my service or my product, I must be very efficient and I must provide the best quality within the best timeframe.

Keeping Calm

"Patience is the virtue of courage".
— BERNARDIN DE SAINT-PIERRE

In a time when speed is something everyone seems to be looking for, it may seem strange to talk about patience. And yet, in each of our lives there will always be things that require time to achieve fulfillment. Reaching our objectives takes time. There are a good number of steps between the time a project starts and the time it can be completed. I must be patient and I must try not to skip over steps that are important. At times, when I hurry too much to reach my goal, I can make costly mistakes and I can jeopardize my project.

Today, I understand the importance of being patient as I travel on the road to success. I may not be able to wait patiently. I may have to move forward each day. However, no matter what happens, I have to take all of the time and I have to make all of the efforts needed to reach my objectives.

Facing Adversity

Today, I admit that the road to success is filled with obstacles. I see that from the time I decide to start a project or do something new, something more important, I am faced with a certain amount of adversity. Of course, the universe never responds immediately to my requests and to my needs. So I must be able to overcome difficult situations, mistakes, problems and misfortunes. I must be able to overcome days when I think that absolutely nothing is going right.

Today, I am prepared to face any kind of adversity that life may bring me. I am aware that genuine success calls for strength and the ability to face and overcome obstacles.

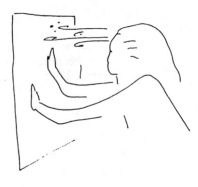

Saying Goodbye to Indifference

Today, I choose to say goodbye to indifference. I choose to escape from the negative influence of the indifference I see in my environment. Today, I choose to surround myself with the kind of people who like my way of thinking and acting. I choose to surround myself with interested and interesting people who want to discover new things and to live new experiences. I also choose to reject my own indifference. And I choose to take action.

I know that indifference eventually leads to quitting and apathy; so when I see that I am beginning to feel indifferent, I change directions. I am an energetic and lively human being and I embrace the present moment. There are so many things I can do. Each day brings me new ideas and I find the inner energy I need to carry out all of my projects and to reach all of my goals.

I Am Perseverant

I have decided to be a perseverant individual because I know that getting the results I want can take a long time in some circumstances. I know that I can stay on course and that I can keep my focus on the objective I want to achieve. Today, I am perseverant because I want to succeed and I want to build a happy and creative life.

My Path

I know that I am an individual being, and so my road is my road alone, my thoughts are mine alone and my actions are mine alone. By recognizing and respecting my individuality, I make my decisions and my actions strong and sure. My individuality also gives me an important responsibility: I am responsible for my own happiness and for my own growth.

I embrace my individuality and I embrace the challenge and the responsibility of travelling my own path. I know that by making myself the most important person in my life and by trusting my inner wisdom and following my own path, I will always live happily and my life will always be full. Such are the laws of the universe. The spiritual being controls the material world. My decisions determine my path. My intentions and my decisions determine my fate.

The more I develop the ability to listen to my inner self, the more I am faithful to who I truly am and the closer I am to my inner harmony. Today, I listen to my inner wisdom and I follow my own path in life.

My Place in the World

Today, I am very aware of the world around me. I see a world filled with activity and movement and as I look around, I experience a certain sense of detachment. I put a certain amount of distance between myself and others so that I can see, hear and understand life on this planet and so that I can begin to understand the individuals who happen to cross my path. Today, I resolve to take my rightful place in our fascinating and wonderful world.

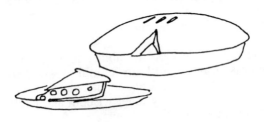

Choosing

I take the time to make choices based on my own needs and on the real needs of the situation. Because of my past, at times I have let myself be controlled by the demands and needs felt by others. I have made hasty choices that have affected my life. Now, I know that I can say "Yes", "No", "Maybe" or "I can't decide right now". I give myself the luxury of choosing at my own pace. Today, I resolve to listen to my inner wisdom and to make choices that are in my own best interests in the long term.

Today, I know that I am the person who chooses. When I realize that most of the things that happen in my life are the results of my own choices and my own decisions, I know that I am in control and I know that I am strong. I can see how my decisions have an impact on my life and how my aptitudes and my life experiences color how I see events and people. When I know that I am accountable, without feeling guilty, I can see what a wonderful person I am and I can see all the possibilities available to me.

Learning to Think for Myself

I have learned to think for myself. Education should lead individuals to use their own intelligence, their own judgement and their own sense of determination. Education should also lead individuals to apply their inner wisdom and to achieve self-fulfillment. Too often, education is perceived as the accumulation of learning and the assimilation of abstract concepts based on outdated principles. I have realized that my greatest asset in this life is knowing how to think for myself and seeking to understand the things and people around me. I respect my ability to learn, to think freely and to know.

Enjoying Freedom

I am a free person. I am free to explore, to take risks, to be spontaneous and to do what I have to do. I know that people are free only to the extent that they are responsible and aware. And so my level of freedom is closely linked to my level of awareness and my ability to accept the results and the consequences of the choices I have made and the choices I intend to make. Freedom of choice and action requires that I be loyal to my inner self and to my principles.

My overall freedom is expressed through my imagination, my ability to choose and my freedom of expression and action.

Reliability

Success is founded on the ability to make things happen, but also on the ability to fulfill promises. At the outset, when we start a new project or a new business, people tend to hesitate before getting too heavily involved with us. They try to determine just how serious we are and just how capable we are of achieving good results. Over time, as we deliver a consistently good product, they begin to trust us. From this point on we can truly begin to grow and to move closer to our objectives.

Today, I know that I have to prove that I am reliable. When I start a new project, I work hard to show that people can count on me. I want to build solid and lasting business relationships so I am not afraid to do all I possibly can to satisfy a client.

All the Good Things in Life

I see how I have set my own limits on the things I can and can't have. For a long time, I felt a deep sense of loss. The attitude that I couldn't do one thing or another, that I couldn't have one relationship or another served only to diminish my ability to have and to keep.

Today, I give myself permission to have. I let things and relationships come to me. How could I think of succeeding if I give myself nothing or if I refuse to embrace what I have?

Today, I give myself permission to have!

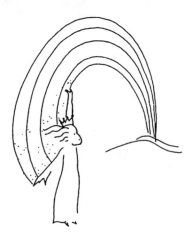

Learning From My Mistakes

I have forgiven myself for the mistakes I've made in the past. The past is the past. I live in the present and I live for the future. I know that if I drag the burden of the past with me, I will be much less free to act and to succeed. So I bid goodbye to the mistakes I've made in the past.

I know that I am here to learn, to grow and to experience life. I am also here to succeed. So I accept the fact that mistakes are part of my life and of the path that will lead me to my objectives. When I make a mistake, I use it to learn and to refocus my attention. I am very aware that I can accomplish nothing by being critical or by feeling guilty. Today, I accept that mistakes are part of my path in life.

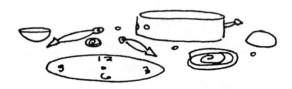

First Impressions

We all know that first impressions can determine whether or not a relationship works out. When we meet a prospective employer or client, the first impression generated by our appearance, our attitude or our approach can spell the difference between success and failure.

Today, I understand the importance of first impressions and I make sure that I am well prepared whenever I meet someone for the first time. When I'm scheduled to meet a new client, I dress well and I prepare all the documents I need well in advance. I try to find out what my new clients may need and when I meet them, I already have a plan of action in mind. And above all, when I meet them I show that I have a very strong commitment to developing a good business relationship based on honesty.

Being True to Myself

"Loyalty is the only currency that keeps its value over time."
— FRANÇOIS GARAGNON

Loyalty is a very noble value. Being loyal in a business or professional relationship demonstrates maturity and our fundamental value as friend or associate. When we are loyal and when we show others that we can be trusted, we can build solid relationships that can withstand the test of time.

But before being loyal to others, we have to be loyal to ourselves, our values, our principles and our own life experiences. Being loyal to ourselves means recognizing our own right to choose. It means recognizing our mistakes and learning from them and it means rewarding ourselves for our successes. Being loyal to ourselves means listening to our hearts and to our inner selves even when the environment we happen to be in may push us to follow group trends. It means having the courage of our convictions and using the power to make choices, to be an individual like no other individual on earth. Today, I am true to myself.

Positive Thinking

I have not always believed in the idea that thoughts could influence my life. I used to believe that positive thinking was a way to hide or cover up the truth. If things were bad, the reason was simply that things were bad and in any event, they were out of my control. But I've discovered that my intentions, my decisions and my way of seeing things have a definite influence on my life experience. Any action and any experience that is mine is based on my own perceptions and my own attitudes.

Today, I resolve to adopt a positive attitude. I resolve to adopt the perceptions and attitudes of a winner. I know that in spite of all the difficulties and all the obstacles I may encounter, I can succeed. I have all the tools, all the talents and all the courage I need to succeed. I can change a failure into a success.

Games

My life had become a perpetual fight for survival. I felt that in general, people were against me and that intentionally or unconsciously, they were trying to stop me from reaching self-fulfillment. In my hard life, there was no real joy, only a few minutes of respite here and there. I felt trapped.

One fine day, I realized that the traps and the trapped feeling were things that I had created for myself. They were something within me, not something exterior to me. In my life, I had created games and I was stuck in the traps of the very same games I had designed. From that time on, I completely changed my way of seeing life, viewing it and playing it as a game.

Today, I see life as a huge playground where there are many different games to play and where I can choose exactly which game I would like to play. When I feel sad or stuck in a rut, I know that I've stopped playing and that I've fallen into my own trap.

Looking at Failure

Behind each no, there is a yes. Behind each failure, there is a success. We can learn much more from our failures than from our successes, because behind failure, there is everything we have failed to understand, everything we have refused to accept or face, everything we have not wanted to see or hear. When I choose to embrace failure and when I am ready to hear the secrets it can tell me, I am open to growth and to learning. Today, I know that eventually, failure is a major victory. Failure brings me back down to earth and pushes me forward on my path to self-fulfillment. When I am faced with failure, I feel curious — never defeated!

Ambition

We often hear that a person can be too ambitious and that ambition has something dangerous and volatile about it. A person who is too ambitious can act aggressively or selfishly. Personally, I believe that ambition and success go hand in hand. I am ambitious when I work hard to achieve my objectives. I am ambitious when I go beyond my limits and when I choose to move forward and grow. I am ambitious when I take on new challenges.

Ambition is good. Being ambitious and wanting to succeed are positive and vital qualities for success. Today, I am ambitious and I am happy to experience the energy that comes from ambition.

Facing Situations

Time has taught me that I have to face situations. I resolve to face difficulties, to solve problems and to see clearly. When I see things clearly, I can act logically until I accomplish what is acceptable to me. When I develop my ability to see things as they are, I am stronger and I escape from my fears. By facing obstacles directly, I am stronger and less dependent on my environment and the various situations that I encounter in life.

Today, I resolve to see things as they really are instead of arguing and trying to impose my own viewpoint. Just as darkness is overcome by light, the truth overcomes lies and deception.

I See the Obvious

"There is rest only for he who seeks.
There is rest only for he who finds."
— RAOUL DUGUAY

Sometimes, I feel upset because I fail to see the things that are in front of my eyes. At times, I've created illusions in my life by believing what I've heard instead of going to see for myself. How many times have I made myself unhappy by believing something I heard instead of believing what I saw.

Now that I have realized this very important fact, I resolve to look around me and to see for myself.

Serving

Today, I understand that serving others doesn't mean lowering myself or showing that I am inferior. Today, I see that dedication and the willingness to serve others are vital qualities that I must develop if I want to succeed. We live in a service-oriented society and everywhere, we see people who hate to serve others. They see serving others as a thankless and very negative idea. Restaurants are often filled with impolite waiters who hate their jobs. Unfortunately, they haven't understood that serving is a privilege and a joy — the best path to personal success.

Today, I take pleasure in serving others because it makes me feel useful and it contributes to my well-being. I know that my willingness to serve will be a determining factor in my personal success.

Being My Own Advisor

*"Do not believe, oh monks, simply because you
have been told something. Do not believe what
your master tells you simply out of respect for
him. But if, after examination and analysis, you
judge the principle to be sound, to hold the
promise of goodness and well-being for the
earth's living beings as a whole, then believe it
and make it your guide."*

— BUDDHA

I have realized that every single person has opinions. These opinions and viewpoints can be very
interesting and can carry the seeds of truth within them. But I have also realized that I must discover things for myself. I have to live through my
own experiences, examine facts myself and in the
end, draw my own conclusions. Our society of
experts and specialists has given us the habit of
not looking for the truth ourselves. Instead, we
tend to trust the judgements, analyses and theories of others. But in the final analysis, I know
that I must live according to my own principles,
my own truths and my own values.

Today, I respect the opinions of others but I base
my decisions, my values and my life on the truths
that I have experienced and tested myself.

I Am the Master of My Destiny

Absolutely nothing forces an individual to live through a particular experience. Beyond the shadow of a doubt, I know that I am entirely free to choose my own fate. Only my intentions, my decisions, my perseverance and my commitment are determinant in the path I choose to achieve my goals. I am the only person who can improve my fate. I am the only person who can predict my future. My decisions determine my path in life and the quality of the experiences it brings me.

I can lose control over my own destiny if I give responsibility or power to a force that is not within me, to a force that goes beyond the realm of my ability to decide and to act.

Today, I know that I am the ultimate master of my fate. At times my actions and decisions may run against the actions and decisions of those around me — but I know that I am in full and total control of my own life.

The Joy of Being My Own Boss

Starting a new business takes a good deal of work and a very well developed sense of responsibility. It means being ready to roll up your sleeves and work very hard and very intelligently for at least a few years before the first truly positive and reassuring results begin to appear. On the other hand, I know of no other activity or no other project that is more satisfying than starting up, managing and overseeing the growth of a business. It is a creative and enriching experience that contributes to growth in all aspects of life.

Today, I know the joy of being my own boss. I embrace the worries, responsibilities, challenges and victories that come from being my own boss. I am the master of my own destiny. Ultimately, I am responsible for my own life.

Change

Some people say that we can change, that we can make our lives completely different. Others say that once formed, our personalities are impossible to change unless we experience a life-changing, traumatic event. There is some truth in both viewpoints. Basically, the personality, identity, behavior, values, attitudes and viewpoints that individuals adopt in life are the result of their learning, culture and temperament. All of these things can change. But each individual's fundamental being, his or her true and spiritual being, cannot change because it is. In simple terms, change is the progressive or sudden discovery of our true being, that being that encourages us to let go of the false and to embrace the truth.

Today, I embrace the person I really am and I resolve to let go of all that is truly not me.

Going with the Flow

People often say that the older you get, the more set in your ways you are. As I grow older, I have resolved to go with the flow. Life, the business world and relationships all call for flexibility. Life asks us to adapt by adopting new outlooks and new behavior patterns. Today, I know that I can adapt. I can go with the flow and I can be gracious without compromising my fundamental values. I want to live in harmony with others and I know that if I am stubborn and set in my ways, I will isolate myself and shut the door on many interesting and positive experiences.

Today, I resolve to develop my ability to adapt because the world around me undergoes constant change. By being open minded, I can use every opportunity available to me and I can shape my attitudes and behaviors to suit any of the situations that life brings me.

When I Was Small

When I was small, my mother used to ask my brother and I to get water from the well. My brother and I used to fight to see who'd have the privilege of doing the chore. When I would reach the well, in the shade of tall fir trees, I would enter a world of water, coolness and tranquility. On my way back, even with my heavy pails filled with cool, fresh water, I would feel strong and energetized.

Today, I remember the important lessons on success that I learned when I was still very young. My parents helped me understand that effort and work deserve to be rewarded. They also taught me that work and responsibilities are something that can be shared. I quickly understood that I had a role to play within my family and that I was expected to take part in the family's life by doing my homework, going to church and doing small jobs around the home. When I look back, I can see that these lessons were very useful and as a result of them, today I realize the value of a good day's work. I know how to shoulder my responsibilities and I can take an active part in the life of my family and of my community.

Sharing Responsibilities

I can see that responsibilities are something that can and should be shared. In my friendships, in my work relationships and in my family life, I understand how important it is to share responsibilities. When I take on too many responsibilities without delegating any of them, I end up helping no one. And similarly, when I let others handle all the responsibilities, I make no contribution to the team's work or to my own self-esteem.

Today, I resolve to do my share and to work with others so that I can achieve equilibrium in my life.

My Moral Code

I am very aware of the importance of having a moral code. I have based my code on truths that have always served me well. I have realized that if I really want to live happily and successfully, I have to apply solid and consistent principles in my life. My rules of behavior and my values are very simple, they direct me when I make decisions and they make it possible for me to live in harmony with myself and others.

My moral code is based on my own experiences, my own observations and my own truths. As long as I follow my own moral code, I know that I can succeed.

I Keep My Promises

"I cling to my ideals and I continue to believe that people are fundamentally good."
— ANNE FRANK

I keep my word and I keep my promises. Before I give my word or before making a promise, I stop and think and I make sure that I can deliver. Once I've thought things out, if I decide to give my word, I know that I can keep it. When I follow this principle, I strengthen my self-esteem and I earn the admiration and respect of all of my friends and colleagues. When I recognize how much weight my word carries and how important it is, I can be reliable and trustworthy. The people who work or live with me know that they can count on me and I know that I can count on myself under all circumstances. And when a problem or a conflict occurs, I will know that I have kept my word and I will be able to see the situation clearly.

I Am an Architect

I know that I am the key player in my life and I know that by accepting all of the situations and all of the problems that I encounter as part of my responsibilities, I increase the control I have on my life and on my fate. Being responsible does not mean taking on the burden of the incompetence or lack of responsibilities that others may show. However, I can act to remove negative people from my life and to surround myself with positive and helpful people. I can also show my support for others and I can be a positive force in their lives.

Responsibility is closely linked to action. When I see that I set things in motion myself, I can take action. When I refuse to take responsibility for what happens, I let other people and the situations in my life take control of me. Even when I see that ultimately, I am not responsible for a particular situation, I know that I am the person in charge of my own feelings and my own thoughts. Responsibility gives me the ability to understand, to act and to succeed.

The Power of My Decisions

I have come to understand the power of my decisions. I decide to take action or not to take action, to be or not to be. Decisions make the world go round. The power of my decisions will always be stronger than material considerations. In the past, at times I have felt that I had to tolerate a given situation and that I had no control over it, but I've come to realize that I am in control of my own life. I make my own decisions. My decisions are extremely powerful. With the power to decide, I can change, I can build or I can destroy anything.

At times I have underestimated the power of my decisions and after deciding something, I've gone back to my old behavior patterns. What I have realized is that behind every new decision, there was an old and even stronger decision that urged me to keep things exactly as they were. So today, I decide and I see that the way my life is, depends on the decisions I have taken in the past. When I want to make a change in my life, I look at the decisions I have taken in the past and based on what I see, I make a new decision.

I Am Responsible for My Own Fate

I recognize that I am entirely responsible for my own fate. I know that outside circumstances have no control over my life. Instead, my intentions, my determination and my actions are what control my life. Today, I resolve to take control of my own fate. I resolve to open new doors, to create new possibilities for myself and to broaden my horizons.

I Congratulate Myself

I congratulate myself on following the path to success. I deserve to succeed and I deserve to be appreciated because I am a good person. I congratulate myself not only on the things that I have done or on my achievements, I also congratulate myself for simply being the person I am. I know that I can count on myself. I deserve love and I deserve respect. I am very aware of the role I play in my own life and the things I do are always intentional. Including solid values in my day-to-day life, bringing self-discipline to my work and working positively with others always calls for a great deal of effort — but I know that the effort I make will be rewarded by an intense, satisfying and fulfilling life.

Looks

In our society, looks are very important. When I look good, I can open many new doors for myself. When I look good, people tend to look at me and to listen to me instead of concentrating on my appearance. Of course, people like to create a particular effect with their appearance. I am aware of the effect I create with my clothing and my physical appearance.

Today, I focus on my appearance. When I make sure that I look good, I send a message on my attitudes and my commitment to success. When I pay attention to the way I look, I draw attention to myself and I earn the respect of people who work with me or who are meeting me for the first time. Today, I pay attention to my looks and I show others that I have the commitment and the resolve to succeed.

The Secret to Prosperity

Today, I can say that I have achieved material wealth. But my situation wasn't always this way. Many years ago, I discovered something very important, something that changed my work relationships: I am interested in making others wealthy. When I stopped worrying about my own prosperity and when I started working actively and intelligently to make others wealthier, my own income began to increase. The rule is simple: when I offer a product or a service that truly contributes to the prosperity, well-being and happiness of others, I am rewarded. But I have to look at where the demand really lies. I have to use my energy to offer things that will contribute to the growth and prosperity of others.

Today, I am committed to making others more prosperous and my commitment brings me satisfaction and success.

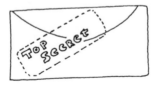

Making Omelettes

"You can't make an omelette without breaking any eggs" is a saying we hear fairly often. At times, we have to make difficult decisions if we want to create something new. People who want to start a business may have to give up the security of a steady income and may have to risk all of their savings. People who want to end a negative relationship may have to break long-time ties and say: "No, it's over."

Today, I am no longer afraid of breaking a few eggs to achieve positive results in my life. I know that I can act positively and I know that I can make the right decisions.

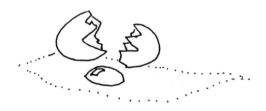

Every Minute is a New Minute

Today, I know that every minute is a new one and that every moment brings with it the possibility of change and renewal. So I can take off my old coat, the coat I used to wear to protect myself from the cold and from abandonment. Scientists say that every cell in our body has the power to regenerate itself. So I can regenerate myself as well. I can change my attitudes, I can change my mind. I can use new glasses to see the world from a completely different viewpoint. I can discover a new truth that will change forever the way I see things and the way I think of them.

Today, I know that every minute brings the opportunity of renewal. Today, I embrace change and I enjoy it. Life is a process of perpetual change. Instead of going against the flow, I will let the current of change carry me gently along.

I Can Solve Problems

I recognize that most problems and most conflicts can be resolved through communication.
When I speak openly and when I let others communicate openly with me, I can overcome my
problems. Misunderstandings and conflicts are
unable to withstand the light of good communication. Every conflict or misunderstanding is the
result of an untruth or something that has gone
unsaid. Therefore, I resolve to speak openly.
Those who are offended by my openness may
have something to hide and in any event, they are
unworthy of my friendship.

I Reap What I Sow

"Continue to sow, for no one knows which seed will grow... perhaps all."

— ECCLESIASTES

I have no doubt on the fact that I reap what I sow. It is absolutely impossible to live an unhealthy and dishonest life without suffering the consequences. Opportunism, greed and dishonesty lead directly to darkness and misfortune. Success demands a firm commitment to justice, love and kindness. I know when I am being honest with myself and I know the difference between good and evil. I can live with lies for a time, but in the long run, lies will make it impossible to live with myself. Eventually, a person who lives with lies seeks to pay for his or her own crimes.

Today, I cherish sound values and I choose the path of honesty and integrity because I am faithful to my own principles and my inner wisdom.

Setting Up a New Business

Have you every noticed that some people are full of ideas for new businesses, but they still have trouble paying their rent? Every time you meet them, they tell you about their latest idea to get rich quick, but they seem to be unable to handle their current responsibilities. They are dreamers who have the energy of impulsiveness and imagination, but they lack the courage and the tenacity to stick to their projects. There is a major difference between them and me. Every time I undertake a project, I finish what I start.

Anybody can set up a new company, have business cards printed, rent offices and buy office furniture. Anybody can get a line of credit from the bank and anybody can have a new telephone line connected. But very few people can carry through with their ideas to create a profitable and lasting business. I know that I belong to that particular minority.

Making and Breaking Ties

I can make or break ties of communication. I am not passive in the communication process. I choose to communicate or not to communicate, and I choose to receive the messages others send me or not to receive them. I am responsible for the communication ties I make and break. It may appear overly simplistic, but the following statement is a fundamental truth: I am free to communicate or not to communicate.

At times, for many different reasons, I choose not to receive the messages others are sending me. I am free to make that choice. At other times, I do want to speak to others, and I am equally free to make that choice. In the same way, there are people I choose not to communicate with at all. I am entirely free to make or break ties.

Today, I choose to make or break ties of communication. And if I want, I can break the ties of communication when what they bring me is negative and when it contributes nothing to my well-being.

The Law of Least Effort

Have you ever heard of the law of least effort? It involves a principle under which a person seeks the best possible results by making the least effort possible. In other words, the idea is to achieve maximum results in exchange for minimal effort. The principle may seem contradictory but nevertheless it is extremely useful in today's world. Look around you: most inventions and technological innovations are based on this very law. Instead of using hours to hand wash laundry, we press a few buttons and use our time elsewhere.

The law of least effort is not based on laziness, but on the idea that there is always a more effective way to do things, one that minimizes our efforts and lets us do more with our time.

Today, I apply the law of least effort as I go about organizing my work. I resolve to optimize my efforts so that I can achieve the best possible results. I give myself the tools I need to cut down on work time and to increase the quality and quantity of production.

Self-Affirmation

Self-affirmation could be described as the art of sending a direct and effective message with the objective of getting a specific result. The process shouldn't involve imposing a message, instead it should be focused on expressing a viewpoint, a request or a need in a given circumstance. Today, I know that I can achieve my goals through self-affirmation.

When I affirm myself, I must avoid any form of anger or aggression. This type of intensity can only break the ties of communication. I must be calm and I must express my request clearly and consistently until I get the result I want. Behind every "no" there is a "yes". I can reach my goals if I am persistent.

Today, I see that I can achieve self-fulfillment and success only through self-affirmation.

Mutual Respect

Mutual respect is a vital aspect of success. How can I surround myself with positive people if I show them no respect and if I fail to give them the freedom to express their own thoughts? How can I express myself freely if I am dealing with people who show me no respect? Each person has an individual life experience, an individual way of looking at things and most importantly, the fundamental right to be themselves under any circumstances.

Today, I encourage positive communication by respecting others and by showing them the respect I have for them.

What School Doesn't Teach Us

There can be no doubt that education is a precious asset that can contribute significantly to our success. But many of the lessons we learn are not taught to us in school, but in everyday life. In the work world, we are faced with the very real demands of jobs to get done, of clients who want us to provide services, of a work team that must work smoothly and of a wide range of practical considerations. In our families, our friendships and our businesses, life teaches us a great many lessons that lead us to harmony and happiness.

Today, I see that life is a lesson and a process of constant improvement. I must be open to life's lessons if I want to improve and succeed. Of course, I expect to achieve my goals without making any mistakes or adjustments. On the other hand, I am always open to new solutions and new approaches.

The Unsaid

"It is absolutely useless to travel a road to preach; unless you preach on the road you travel."
— SAINT FRANCIS OF ASSISI

We all learn that an important part of communication is nonverbal. We communicate with bodily and facial expressions, with hand gestures, with looks, with sighs, etc. Actions also communicate important messages. Ultimately, we must rely more on actions than on words because words are easy to say, but harder to put into action.

I evaluate the people around me on the basis of their actions much more than on the basis of their words. Reliable and honest individuals keep their word and carry out their plans to the end. Less honest individuals can talk a lot and say all sorts of things, but they get very little done. I want to be an honest person who is worthy of trust and so I seek to carry out my projects as planned and to live up to my commitments. To protect my self-esteem, I apply my principles and I am true to my word.

Opinions

Every one of us has opinions. Often, they can be very interesting and very useful. You can find people who will tell you how to raise your children, how many plants you can grow in your garden, how you can settle your financial problems and which vitamins you should take after breakfast. But there is a very big difference between someone who knows what they are saying and someone who is simply expressing an opinion. Opinions are a dime a dozen on any street corner, but advice from someone who has been successful in a particular area is worth much, much more.

I am always interested in the views of others. They stimulate me and they help me look at things from different angles. But I do not base my decisions on the opinions other people give me. Instead, I listen to what they have to say, I analyze it and I make my own decision. And sometimes, I consult someone who has more experience than I have and I ask for advice.

My Colleagues

Work can involve many stressful situations. In spite of stress, it is important to maintain good relationships with my colleagues. If I give into my emotions and create a situation of conflict or if I criticize a colleague because of a mistake, I may hurt our ability to work together.

Today, I see how important it is to maintain positive relationships with my colleagues. I resolve to create a positive work climate that encourages cooperation and mutual help and I refuse to get involved in conflicts or to react angrily or negatively. If a colleague's behavior hurts me or the quality of my work, I find an effective and diplomatic way to solve the problem.

Quality, Quality, Quality

Today, we talk about quality control as if quality was the new obsession for every business that exists on the planet. But at second glance it's easy to see that quality is a rather vague notion and what it really means is offering a consistent product. For me, quality means reliability, usefulness, durability and value. A product or a service shows quality when it meets the client's need and when it is based on a genuine effort to produce something that is truly useful and reliable.

We need to offer clients as much as we can. We need to give them all they want and all that they may be looking for in a product or a service — and even more. A quality product or service must also be available at a price that is fair or lower than the prices set by the competition. Each company has the responsibility of rationalizing its operations and organizing production to provide products of consistent quality.

Today, I know that my success depends entirely on my ability to offer a product or a service of superior quality. I know that a quality product will satisfy my client and at the same time, it will make me proud of my work and will help me along the road to success in my particular area of expertise.

The Customer is Always Right

"The client is always right" is an expression that we all often hear. The idea is that businesses should focus on customers satisfaction and they should do all they can to encourage customers loyalty. Theoretically, it is extremely important to respect this principle. But at the same time, we all have to beware of people who want to take advantage of our commitment to customer satisfaction. At times people can mistreat the members of our organization simply for the pleasure it brings them. But fundamentally, the golden rule that the client is never wrong can be crucial to business operations.

Today, I seek to satisfy my customers and I consider that they are always right because I want to develop positive business relationships. When a customer is dissatisfied, regardless of the reason, I do all that I can to solve the problem.

Building Long-Term Relationships

Success is based on long-term relationships. Like a good wine, a relationship improves over time. Eventually, each person in a relationship comes to understand how the other one works. They share values and they contribute to each other's success. I protect long-term relationships and I nurture them whenever I can.

Today, I see that my success depends on my relationships and I seek to maintain them over the long term. When I maintain relationships over time, I can build a strong network of allies who can share in my commitment to growth.

The American Dream

Since it became the strongest nation in the world, the United States have been accused of a very possible wrong. America is special because it can offer anyone (in theory) the opportunity to succeed. There is something healthy and honest in a culture that offers even the most underprivileged the right to dream that one day, they will be in a much better position in life. The American dream is what makes the America so much different from other, more stagnant societies. And when ordinary people have no access to dreams and have no conviction that their lives can be better, they stop believing in a system and they begin to look for ways to overthrow it.

Today, I follow the American example by believing that I can improve my life. I dream of the day when I will be financially independent and when my lifestyle will be enviable in the eyes of others. I follow the American example by taking action and doing the things I know will make my dreams come true. Each day, I work hard and I keep my eyes focused on my objectives and my ultimate dreams.

Life's Instruction Manual

For a long time, I searched for an operator's manual to tell me how to live my life. I wanted instructions that could help me understand and improve my ability to succeed. There are many interesting approaches to life and there are many books that deal with personal development. But I have come to realize that I must discover my own approach and my own truths. I can definitely use the theories and the strategies developed by the world's great thinkers, but I have to find my own road to success.

Today, I develop my own strategies and my own approaches so that I can be successful. I base my approach on sound values and on the commitment to serve others and to do good. I am not alone in my quest for a life of harmony and along the way, I can find friends who share my values and my will to succeed.

The Spiritual Side of Work

"Generally speaking, accomplishment implies a certain type of power, of control, of mastery, of commitment and of belief that a particular individual can accomplish a specific task. On a higher level, it does not mean simply accomplishing a task, but also being aware that the task has been accomplished. Indeed, at the highest level, accomplishment is probably the feeling that one has contributed to something, which in itself makes the task worthwhile."

— CHARLES L. WHITFIELD

Beyond any other consideration, work enables the individual to rise to the highest ranks in society. But work also has a spiritual side to it. By working, I recognize that I am the architect of my own life. I am aware that there is always something to do and something that I can contribute to. By working, I strengthen my relationship with myself and with others. Work is virtuous because it brings me pride and freedom.

Following the Japanese Example

The Japanese surprised and impressed the entire world by becoming a global economic power within only a few decades. Our captains of industry, economists and heads of state were so taken aback by the emergence of Japan as an economic force that for a time, they did everything they could to prevent the Japanese from entering our markets. But gradually, manufacturers began to adopt the new standards applied by the Japanese. The Japanese secret is not as complicated as we tend to think. While Americans and Europeans were compromising on quality to cut costs and to develop throw-away products, the Japanese were turning out quality products with a long life cycle and making them available at lower prices. Consumers reacted by choosing quality.

Today, I know that if I want to succeed, I have to satisfy my customers by offering them quality work. I can follow the Japanese example by working efficiently and effectively to bring a better product to the market. If I want to take my rightful place in the modern economy and if I want to build a loyal customer base, I have to offer the best quality I can.

The Artist

I've always believed that I was an artist
And with my brush, I could paint the world.

I've always believed that I was a singer,
And with my music, I could tell you how much I
loved you.

I've always believed that I was a sculptor,
And with my hands, I could mold rock into something beautiful.

I've always believed that I was a poet,
And with my words, I could change the world.

The Value of Money

At one point in my life I realized that basically, money could be used in two ways: we can use it to acquire goods and services, or we can use it to generate increase in value*. When we use money to consume, our constant concern is the source of the money we spend. When we set out on the process of creating value, either by creating a product or a service that others need, we are our own source of prosperity. We add to our inherent value and money becomes a secondary issue.

Today, I see money as a means to create value. I invest in creating a product or a service that fills a need. And when I do, I can transform money into a work tool and I can stop seeing it as an end in itself.

---

* We increase the value of a product, when it has been transformed into something useful. For example, transforming wax into a candle increases it's value.

Putting Yourself in Other People's Shoes

"Tolerance is the charitable expression of intelligence."

— JULES LEMAÎTRE

Tolerance is giving other people the right to be, to have their own ideas, customs and beliefs, to like whatever reflects their own tastes and to live and think differently than I may.

Tolerance begins at the core of any society: the family. It begins with parents who watch their toddlers taking their very first steps, who patiently share their knowledge and their life experience, who encourage their children and teach them to be perseverant. Children need time to learn and understand; knowledge and wisdom is something acquired gradually. Children remember precisely what we say and how we say it. As proof, think of the hatred that is passed down from generation to generation in some instances.

Today, I realize that I must be tolerant if I want to create harmony in the workplace. Team work is a factor that will always be important to my success and I keep an open mind when I am confronted with the ideas, personalities and behaviors of people who are different from me.

The Conditions for Satisfaction

I have learned that it is very useful to set down the terms and conditions for satisfaction before beginning a project. For me, the process involves defining what can make the client feel satisfied and what he or she expects from me. I also determine what remuneration will be given for a job well done. Of course, I may encounter unforeseen circumstances along the way and they may require negotiating. But by beginning with the step of defining what satisfaction involves, I can work with total peace of mind because I know what is expected of me. The process lets me analyze the situation and to plan my work from the outset.

Today, before I begin a project or a contract, I take the time to define the terms and conditions of satisfaction with my customers. I eliminate any source of conflict or misunderstanding from the outset and I focus my energy on the work I have to do.

Going Further

"If at first you don't succeed, try, try again."

Persevere is a word whose stem comes from the Latin for "severe" (severus), meaning inflexible. Someone who is perseverant never quits. People who have been successful in their lives all have something in common: perseverance. Their success stories show consistent effort, persistence in difficult situations and the will to go on, even when the temptation to give in to discouragement has been very great.

Today, I know that perseverance comes from within. It is not something I can find outside myself. Even when friends offer me encouragement, nothing can replace my own perseverance.

Perseverance is the marathon runner who refuses to give in to exhaustion before he or she has crossed the finish line. It is standing up to adversity. It is refusing to give in even when all seems lost.

Being Genuine

"Strength is expressed through ferocious honesty with oneself. Only when one has the courage to face things as they are, without illusion or deception, can the light of truth spring forth to guide us on the right path."

— THE I CHING

Honesty is the quality we associate with individuals who never seek to rob or cheat others. Originally, honesty was a notion associated with honor. Someone honest was a fair individual, worthy of consideration and respect.

Honesty is a crucial quality for anyone who wants to succeed. We must be ferociously honest with ourselves. We must look at things as they truly are and we must rely on ourselves as we carry out our work projects. Being successful means being sure that we have done all we possibly could in every single activity we undertake and it means keeping our word. Success means confronting difficult situations and problems and finding the best solutions available to us. When I am honest and sincere with others, I earn their respect and their trust. They know that they can count on me because I am always honest with them.

Creating Harmony

"Our lives are punctuated with kind words and gracious gestures. We feed on expressions marking basic courtesy, such as: "Excuse me, please." Impoliteness, the negation of the sacrament of consideration, is yet another characteristic of our society, focused on money, deprived of spirituality, perhaps even deprived of the pleasure of living."

— ED HAYS

Kindness is easy to include in the way I interact with the people I encounter in my day-to-day life. I can be kind to those who cross my path. By being kind, I create harmony around me, I recognize that the people around me are important and I show them my respect and my love. People react more positively to kindness. They want and look for kindness in all of their interaction with others. Kindness opens the heart and the soul. It enables communication and affection to emerge and flourish. By being kind, I sow the seeds of love and harmony.

Doing Groundwork

Starting a business or a project takes groundwork. Groundwork involves analyzing every factor that can contribute to my success. Groundwork minimizes the risks inherent in the undertaking and it lets me identify what I need to succeed. Depending on the nature or the scope of the project, doing the groundwork it calls for can take a few days or, in some cases, a few years. Groundwork paves the way to success. It may involve learning something new in the workplace or going back to school to retrain.

Today, before beginning a project, I do the groundwork. I do the groundwork it takes to plan the various steps in the work process and I do the groundwork it takes to prepare for the challenges I will have to take on. I do the mental, financial and emotional groundwork it takes to meet each of the project's demands. When I do the groundwork a project involves, I increase my chances of succeeding.

Developing a Winning Formula

Today, I know that to succeed in business I need to develop and use a winning formula. Developing a winning formula involves several steps: identifying market needs, developing a product or a service that is designed to fill a clearly identified need, testing the product or service in my target market, changing the product or service based on test results, delivering the product, analyzing sales results to determine whether the product or service achieves its original objectives.

Then the winning formula must be refined and reinforced based on the specific needs of my market. I see that when I develop a winning formula, I am on my way to success. I take no chances: I use objective standards and I apply a strategy designed to test my business hypotheses.

Determination

Today, I know that determination has its rewards. The universe respects and embraces only those who show determination. Determined individuals who refuse to give in to appearances, mediocrity, dishonesty and cowardice will not be swallowed up in the torment that will emerge when the physical universe gives way and releases the truths it holds.

Life is an Adventure

"Today, I live life to the fullest; I embrace the adventure that is life. I no longer run away from risks. For too long, my life was marked by the boredom that comes with a rigid routine. Because I searched for security, I created a routine that robbed my life of all excitement. Today, I want to explore and to broaden my physical, mental and spiritual horizons. I want to enjoy the euphoria that comes with new experiences."

— ROKELLE LERNER

I believe that I can create the life I want. I don't have to compromise. I can be happy and fulfilled in all aspects of my life. When I treat life like a wonderful adventure, I open the door to new things and new experiences. I can build a new life with a completely different set of building blocks!

Today, I resolve to set out on the adventure of life and I know that I can be happy.

Being Happy

"The real way to be happy is to love your work and to find joy in it."
— FRANÇOISE DE MOTTEVILLE

I have realized that work can be a game, that it can be a source of pleasure and joy. I don't wait for my work to be done before I have fun. I have fun while I work. I don't believe that life begins when you retire. I can live and I can be happy while I am still working. When I work I build, I find fulfillment, I express myself.

Today, I resolve to enjoy my work.

Doing What I Feel is Necessary

"Put all your heart, your spirit, your mind and your soul into the smallest of your gestures. Such is the secret to success!"
— SWAMI SIVANADA

I am aware that ultimately, I must rely on my own judgement and I must do what I feel is necessary. I can listen to the advice of my friend, my family, experts in various field, but ultimately, I must live with the consequences of my acts. So I must find within myself the specific responses to the situations and problems facing me.

I must be able to find my way in society. I must develop my own formula, my own recipe. I can borrow elements from here and there, but I must create my own strategies.

Today, I am happy when others share their advice and opinions with me but I know that in the end, I must listen to my heart and do what I feel is necessary.

Simple Work

"When we do tasks over and over again, we begin to recognize the natural cycles of growth and deterioration, of birth and death; thus, we realize the dynamic order of the universe. 'Simple' work is work that is in harmony with the universal order that we perceive in the natural environment."

— FRITJOF CAPRA

I believe there is something very nurturing in the simple work each of us does every day. I find equilibrium in simple tasks. When I do housework, iron or wash dishes, I feel that I am putting my life in order. These small daily tasks require very little intellectual effort. I can do them while I think of other things that are of concern to me. I can do them as I plan other activities. Simple work is a form of meditation for me. Today, I enjoy carrying out simple tasks and as I do, I put my life in order.

Solving Problems

To succeed, I realize that I must solve the problems that I encounter along life's path. If I try to avoid them, sooner or later they resurface and I have to work even harder to solve them because of my initial resistance. But if I develop an attitude that lets me embrace problems as if they were old friends, I never feel that a situation is hopeless. I can see a problem as an obstacle or a barrier, or I can choose to see it as something completely different. I can see problems as interesting variations of a game, things that add excitement to my life. I can look at problems as something positive because they help me grow, they help me go forward on the road to success and they make me stronger.

Today, I see that the key to my success lies in my ability to solve problems. Instead of running away from problems, I embrace them.

who's spoiled if you do

— MERYL STREEP

...o what is crucial in life: buildin... person who is responsible for my life an... ...ell-being. When I work, I find fulfillment. I contribute to society. I am entirely responsible for the place I make for myself within my family, within my community and in the world. When I let others work for me, I lose that place. Today, I roll up my sleeves and I work gladly.

I can get up every morning to earn my living. That, in itself, is very honorable. But I am capable of doing more. With my work, my intelligence and my creativity, I can build a greater future, I can found a company and I can bring it to the point where it can survive when I am gone. I am here to create links, to go beyond my limitations, to bring something that the world didn't have before I came along. Today, my work lets me build something greater, something new, something beautiful that can contribute to the lives of the beings who share this planet with me.

Accepting Help from Others

"I had decided to work alone. I would take care of myself. I didn't need anybody else's help. My decision was based on the idea that I could get the best results if I worked alone, that others would just slow me down. Of course, I felt this way because of the negative experiences I had had in the past. And based on these experiences, I decided to withdraw. With time, I realized that I could work alone only for a certain period of time. Eventually, I saw that I had to accept help from others."

— M. GEORGE

Working in a group can be a wonderful experience. On the other hand, it calls for good communications, cooperation and courtesy. The rewards of group work are tremendous. Groups can build something together. They can accomplish great things. They can share unbelievably positive experiences.

Today, I know that I can work alone or I can work as part of a group. I am open to cooperation and to team work.

Not Thinking About Retirement

"If I am unable to find pleasure in washing the dishes or if I want to get the job over with as quickly as I can so that I can sit back down at the table to eat my dessert, I am equally unable to enjoy my dessert! As I pick up my fork, I am thinking about the next task that awaits me and the dessert's texture and taste and all the pleasure it brings fade into the background. I will always be dragged into the future and I will never be capable of enjoying the present."

— THICH NHAT HANH

Society believes in a concept that goes something like this: *By working intelligently and saving my money, I can retire when I'm still young and then I can really begin to enjoy life.* This way of thinking is unproductive because it shifts our focus to the future and forces us to turn away from the magic of the present moment. Work isn't something we do while we wait for retirement. Work is real life, here and now.

Today, I like the fact that my days are filled with activities, meetings and commitments. For me, real life — the only life — is now. I wouldn't change the busy life I have today.

The Courage to Succeed

It takes as much energy to succeed as it does to handle a failure. There is as much work in success as there is in failure. There are as many difficulties in success as there are in failure. I have realized that expanding or staying small takes the same amount of active work. When we fail to focus our efforts and our energy on achieving our goals, we waste an astonishing amount of energy resisting what occurs naturally. Individuals naturally seek to find fulfillment and to experience success in their undertakings. And it takes a great deal of effort to fight our own success.

I can see that success calls for a certain amount of courage — the courage to look at the unwise decisions and the obstacles we may have put on the road to our success. Such an exercise requires a great deal of wisdom and honesty. When we decide to take stock of our limitations, our unwise decisions and our barriers, already we have managed to open the door to success. Success requires the courage to live life more fully, to embrace a more demanding type of life. It requires that we move past the limitations that we may have experienced at some point in the past.

Today, I use my courage to move towards the successful achievement of my goals.

Business Ethics

"I do not know what fate has in store for you, but of one thing I am sure of: the only individuals among you who will experience true happiness are those who will seek and find a way to serve others."

— ALBERT SCHWEITZER

The reality of the business world can be hard to face because while some business people are very aware of business ethics, for others it is completely unimportant. They behave ethically when things are going well, but when harder times come along, they forget about ethics. This attitude leads directly to mediocrity and very often, even failure. Without a solid ethical base, a business can't prosper. Successful businesses and individuals have the support of their customers, their suppliers, their banks and their employees or colleagues.

In business, behaving ethically simply means offering a product or a service that contributes to the good of a customer or of society as a whole. It also means offering a product or a service of good or superior quality at a fair price.

I know that if I want to succeed, I must apply the basic rules of ethics in every aspect of my work.

The Key to Success

"If you want to compress something, begin by letting it expand. He who begins by asking, asks for too much, and in the end, succeeds in nothing."
— THE I CHING

There are not a thousand and one ways to succeed in one's professional life. First, choose a field you like and then work hard for a good number of years so that you fully understand all of the aspects it involves. By setting down solid roots in your chosen field and by taking your rightful place in it, you will earn the respect and cooperation of your peers. Changing directions and fields of interest often can lead to self-discovery, but it does not necessarily lead to success.

Today, I take the decision to continue working in my chosen field because I know that I will succeed in taking my rightful place within it.

The Power of Dreams

I can create a mental image of the goals I want to reach. If I want a particular result, I must imagine it as if it were something that I have already achieved. Such is the power of my dreams. I can imagine my future. I can imagine the kind of life I want to live and the kind of situations I want to experience. I can use my mental images as a guide.

If I have no goals and no dreams, how can I be sure that I am moving closer to self-fulfillment? I can use my imagination to guide my actions.

Today, I use my dreams to guide and inspire me.

The Work of Others

"A hundred times a day, I tell myself that my inner and outer life depends on the work of other men, living and dead, and that I must strive to give as much as I have received and will continue to receive."

— ALBERT EINSTEIN

I have realized that I must work every day to earn my place in society. I cannot be content with a life of dependence on the work of others. It may be very tempting to live at the State's expense, simply out of frustration or a sense of resignation. But I work not only because I want to earn my living. I work to strengthen my self-esteem, to come into contact with others, to contribute to the well-being of others. Today, I recognize the importance of doing my share.

What I Do is Important

*"The smallest little task in day-to-day life con-
tributes to the overall harmony of the universe."*
— SAINT THERESA OF LISIEUX

Every task, every job that contributes to the overall harmony of the universe is good. Every trade
has its value. The window-washer, the housewife,
the plumber, the physicist — all play a role in
creating harmony in social relationships.

Today, I am proud of the work I do. I am happy to
contribute to the harmony of the universe.

One Day at a Time

Just as you build a house by laying a foundation, we build our future with one action, one task at a time, and one day at a time. Today I have the opportunity of taking one more step towards my goal. I keep my goal in mind and I work hard at achieving it. I don't get discouraged because I know that satisfaction comes from a day filled with work well done. I take pleasure in doing my very best in all that I undertake and in this way, I increase my happiness and my sense of pride.

We Succeed When We're Happy

Happiness is a good indicator of the success in our lives. When we are happy, we feel confident and relaxed. We can look at life from an optimistic but also detached point of view. We are efficient in our work and positive in our communications and our interactions with others. Happiness and success go hand in hand. I have a recipe for being happy:

—I never do to others what I would not want them to do to me;
—I pursue my dreams and my objectives passionately and persistently;
—I make my values an important part of my day-to-day life; I respect others and I comply with the laws of society;
—I share the fruits of my success;
—I am always willing to lend a helping hand to a friend, a loved one or a colleague;
—I respect my commitments and I keep my word;
—I take an active part in my family's life and in my community's life;
—I am faithful in my relationships;
—I am an efficient worker.

I use this simple recipe to be happy and it brings me only good things.

Earning Professional Respect

I believe that an important part of self-esteem comes from whether or not we have earned respect within our chosen profession. Respect attracts respect. Honesty attracts self-confidence and self-assurance. Consistency and politeness attracts camaraderie and creates a positive climate in the workplace. Cooperation and understanding attracts friendship and love. Each day, I take a close look at my behaviors and attitudes towards others. I refuse to tolerate inefficiency, cheating or sabotage, but I love to work with individuals who sincerely want to learn and improve.

All of us are in the same boat and most of our concerns are the same. So I respect the people I work with and I try to help them to help me. I want to be a respected member of my profession, so I act accordingly. Although I do set limits, I help and respect those who work for me and with me.

The Value of Mistakes

"Children aren't afraid to try new things; they aren't afraid of failing or of trying again. So why are we, as adults, so obsessed with failures — our own and those of our children? Why is it so hard to let our children be average, to let them make mistakes? Why do we feel so much anxiety as soon as we make a mistake?"

— JUDY FORD

We believe, perhaps unconsciously, that we should always succeed and look good in every situation. This belief limits our ability to succeed because it makes it difficult for us to recognize and accept our mistakes. Furthermore, the need to succeed at all costs hinders our ability to act freely and spontaneously.

Today, I give myself the freedom to act and I am prepared to accept my mistakes. I know that if I make a mistake, I can recognize it and I can adjust my future behavior. I see that spontaneity and freedom of action are more important than appearances.

The Folly of Money

We mistakenly confuse success with financial success. Even though most of us admit that money isn't the only thing that can make us happy, we still feel that we'd be happier if we had more of it. Most of us dream of winning the lottery, at least once in a while. On that day, all of our problems would magically disappear! In fact, we spend a great deal of time thinking of money.

I have spent much of my life worrying about money. I felt that no matter what I did, I was never earning enough, I was never rich enough. It seemed to me that I could never have a big enough bank account for me to make all of my wishes come true. And then, at one point, after a lot of hard work, I began to earn much more than I could spend. For the first time, my income went well beyond my ability to buy things and spend money. And suddenly a feeling of calm and serenity came over me. For the first time in my life, I was free of the feeling that I would never be able to make my wishes come true. From that time on, I was free from the folly of money and I stopped focusing my attention on the acquisition of material and financial wealth.

What Do I Expect From Life

It can be interesting to look at the expectations we have when it comes to life. I can wonder what do I expect from relationships? What do I want to achieve during my time in this world? What do I expect from myself? When I see my expectations more clearly, I can identify the kinds of experiences and relationships I want to create for myself and the kinds of projects I want to get involved in. I start out with the idea that I can have the kind of life that I truly want. I no longer feel that life will be a series of compromises.

Today, I take a close look at what I expect from life. I know that I can build the kind of relationships I want and I can create the life I see as ideal. I put an end to the compromises I was willing to make because I thought that I would never find what I really wanted in life. I put an end to the notion that I must live a life that others consider to be acceptable. I can work on making my dreams come true and I can build the life that I want in this world.

My Dreams

"With both feet on the ground, you can't learn much about free falling."
— JOYCE MAYNARD

I believe that if I didn't have dreams, my life would be dull and routine. And furthermore, if I have no dreams, how will I know if I am getting any closer to my ideal life? Where will I find the inspiration to carry on and to build a better life?

Today, I nurture my dreams. Today, I let my imagination run wild and I see my ideal future before my eyes. This ability to create my own dreams gives me hope and inspiration each day. I know that the pleasure lies not in the realization, but in the building of my dreams and in the road that I travel to make them come true.

Dreaming means taking risks because a dream that involves no action is simply an illusion. So each day, I work at making my dreams a reality. For me, there can be no other way to live.

Today, I dream and I look for ways to make my dreams come true.

Taking a Stand

To succeed, we must take a stand. If we believe that we can start something and stop along the way, if we don't really like it, we will never be truly dedicated to the undertaking and we will not be successful in achieving our goals. Success calls for an unreserved and unconditional commitment. We must take a stand and say: "*I am in this until the end, no matter what happens*". It's a question of determination, but more importantly, it's a question of total and complete commitment. When I take a stand and when I decide to go ahead with something, I send a powerful message throughout the universe. If I reserve the right to back out or to give up along the way, then that is the message I will be sending to the universe.

Today, I take a stand. I decide to move forward in the profession I've chosen and to bring total commitment and dedication to my work. I refuse to consider the possibility of questioning my choice at a later point in time. I am here to stay, no matter what happens.

Generosity

I see very clearly the value of generosity in a world that is too often cold, rude and austere. Generosity is a soft light that shines from the heart to light the path of others. Today, I know that I have nothing to lose by being generous. There are only winners in the game of generosity — never any losers. How can I succeed if I have no interest in the success of others? How can I reap the benefits of my success while I see others experiencing hardship? How can I grow and see others fail to grow?

Today, I understand that the universe is not a one-way street. If I want to win, I also have to support others in victory. By being generous, I give back a little of what the universe has given me and I contribute to the success of others.

My Natural Kindness

Today, I let my natural kindness shine through. Kindness creates small spaces for joy and freedom in my life and in the lives of others. When I am good and benevolent, I rise above the fight for survival and I reach a much nobler and more enriching level of action. Today, I am fully aware and I resolve to create a kinder and gentler world.

Kindness has nothing to do with the fear of not being loved; it stems from a generous heart and an open mind. I am not kind only because I want others to recognize my kindness. Instead, I seek to show my true colors in all aspects of my life.

Goodness, love and generosity are the instruments I use to improve my fundamental being. These small tools exist only because of the suffering and the many problems facing us in this world. In truth, goodness, love and generosity are qualities that spring from my fundamental kindness. I need only listen to myself to hear the voice of kindness.

I am a fundamentally good person and I try to be kind under all circumstances. I need only listen to myself to hear the voice of kindness.

Refusing to Compare

I have come to understand that the process of comparing ourselves to others contributes nothing to our personal success. I must travel my own road, make my own choices and live my own experiences. Above all, I must take the time I need to fully grasp all of the steps I take along my life's path. When I compare myself to others, I tend to ask myself the wrong questions and I feel disappointed or impatient.

Today, I no longer compare myself to others. I accept the fact that I am a different individual and that I must pursue my own objectives. I focus my attention on my work and my achievements and regardless of what others do, I do what I know will make me happy.

The Reward of Work Well Done

Today, I know that there is a reward for work well done. It's not a matter of money, but a question of honor and personal satisfaction. When we work hard and when we give the best of ourselves to the task at hand, we get more pleasure and more satisfaction from our jobs.

If I bring dedication and commitment to my work, I will be rewarded in many ways. How can I lose and how can I feel unhappy if I work at something I like and if I do it well? How can I be poor and unhappy if I work with a positive outlook and if I focus on precision and quality?

The Pyramid of Prosperity

It seems that there are three kinds of people in the business world: 1) those who sell their own work for a salary; 2) those who sell the work done by their employees, in the form of products or services; 3) those who manage intellectual property (who issue licenses, patents, copyrights and permissions to use certain ideas, formulas, concepts, technologies or methods and receive fees in exchange). Those who control the world today are those who control and manage intellectual property — the world we live in is a world of ideas, not a world of objects.

People who sell their work for a salary are limited by the number of hours in a day and by the amount of money the market is willing to pay for their work. People who sell the work of others, as products or services, are more likely to be prosperous but are limited by the material constraints of production and distribution. People who manage intellectual property have no constraints because they grant rights and permissions and receive fees in return without taking any risks.

Our Greatness

"The human being is an aspect of the great oneness that we call the universe, with limitations in time and in space. The human perceives his being, his ideas and his feelings as something separate from the rest, a sort of optical illusion of his conscience. This illusion is our prison, limiting our desires and our affection only to those around us. Our task consists of freeing ourselves from this prison by widening the circle of our compassion to embrace all living beings and all of Nature."

— ALBERT EINSTEIN

With time, I came to understand that I can be good or kind and that I shouldn't be afraid of giving, sharing, and trusting others. I used to think: "If I'm good, they'll take advantage of me and they'll want more and more from me." This attitude limited my ability to give. I could not give freely, whether it was money, material goods, my time or my love. I used to hold back.

Today, I know that I have an unlimited ability to share with others.

Integrity in Business

Many people think that integrity and honesty are secondary considerations in the business world. When the situation requires it, they are willing to compromise on quality, take undue advantage of the customer, cheat the State by hiding part of their business income, etc. They operate on the notion that "what you don't know doesn't hurt you". But reality is very different. Individuals who do not adopt the values of integrity and honesty in business can never prosper. They are doomed to perpetuating a lie and eventually, they fail.

Various factors contribute to making integrity a crucial element in business and in life as a whole. At times we may be successful in covering up petty crimes and the situation may last for a while. But by acting this way, we know in our hearts that we are not being completely honest. That knowledge limits our power to take positive action and hurts our growth.

Today, I know that honesty and integrity are sound values. They guide me in my behaviors and attitudes and in the end, they lead to peace of mind, joy and prosperity.

Paying Attention to Others

"The nicest gift anyone can give to someone is a deep attention to the fact that they exist."
— SUSAN ATCHLEY EBAUGH

I keep in mind that each person who crosses my path is a spiritual being, a soul that will share my life for a time. My relationships involve human beings, not simply bodies. So when I communicate with someone, I recognize the true being in front of me.

With this recognition, I can behave in a loving and respectful way towards others. I treat them as if they were of very great value. I speak to the true being and not to the personality or the attitude. I don't let others bully me, but I try to act cordially and kindly towards people of all nationalities and all ages.

Succeeding Step by Step

Today, I know that before I can run, I have to learn to walk. When I want to achieve a specific objective, I know that I have to go about it one step at a time. In business, a common reason for failure is trying to do things too quickly and in so doing, we skip important steps. Success involves gradual progress based on consolidation. I must move forward gradually, completing each step of my project before I begin the next one. Consolidation requires that the next action I take in a project rest on building blocks I have laid down during previous steps. I create stability when I complete each individual step of a project carefully and meticulously.

Today, I move toward my goals one step at a time. I take the time to consolidate each level of development before I move on to the next stage in my work. I begin and finish projects that I know I am fully capable in making a success; I increase my abilities and my resources before I decide to move on to more challenging and more ambitious types of projects.

Strength and Weakness

"Through sheer luck, a man may reign over the world for a little while; but by virtue of love and goodness, he can reign over the world forever."
LAO TZU

Many people still don't understand that it is impossible to dominate, control or enslave people using force and aggression. Our societies are increasingly violent and we struggle to settle our differences by using intimidation and violence. Violence breeds violence. Force leads to a reaction of equal magnitude. Such is the structure of the universe. Only goodness, kindness and compassion can tear down the walls that separate us.

Now I see that goodness is the way that leads to the highest levels of consciousness and action. I turn away from intimidation and aggression and I adopt attitudes and behaviors based on love and compassion.

Loving, Learning and Growing

"We who have lived in concentration camps remember people who gave comfort to others, along with their last morsel of bread. Perhaps they are few in number, but they are the proof that you can rob a man of everything save one: the last of human freedoms, the freedom to choose his attitude, regardless of the circumstances, to choose his path."

— VICTOR FRANKL

Now I know that I have the complete choice to live a life of greatness or a life of smallness. I have all the elements in hand to make enlightened choices. I can choose to be good, honest and sincere or I can choose to be selfish, indifferent and superficial. I can choose between the superficial world of appearances or the world of truth and light. I am not here to accumulate material wealth or to honor my physical body. I am here to love, to learn and to grow.

Loyalty

I give my loyalty judiciously. Loyalty is the ability to support and share responsibility with a friend, an associate, a spouse or a group. It is a very noble quality. When you show loyalty you are saying: "No matter what happens, I will be by your side to bring you my help and my support." I want to be a person others can rely on, even in difficult situations. When I give my allegiance to someone, I never take it back. But like respect, loyalty must be earned. I am vigilant and I do not give my loyalty unquestioningly or blindly. First, I make sure that the person in question deserves it. Usually, I know whether a person or a group deserves my loyalty after observing them over a period of time and after sharing experiences with them. I remember that I have the choice and the right to give my loyalty to the individuals and the groups of my choice.

Identifying My Allies

I have learned to identify my allies. I analyze the behavior and attitudes of the people around me and I choose to be around those who truly contribute to my well-being. I have also understood that I must stay away from those who slow me down and bring chaos into my life. I will not be intimidated. I am a free and responsible individual.

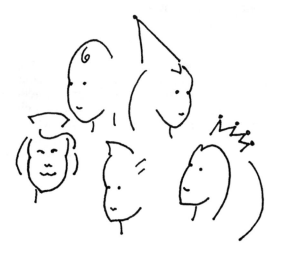

Serving Others

"No joy equals the joy of serving others."
— SAI BABA

Most of us have lost the notion of serving others. To some extent we associate serving others with a form of degradation or slavery. We live in an age of liberation. But our overly individualistic outlook results in isolation and spiritual hardship. There can only be one true goal for people living within a society: serving others. A lifetime of serving ourselves is sterile and fruitless. A lifetime of serving our families, our communities, our businesses, our planet, is the only true life.

Serving does not mean being a slave or acting as someone else's inferior. Serving means using my talents and my resources for the greater good of all. When I serve, I find self-fulfillment, I create harmony and I become a full-fledged member of humanity.

The Job Market

Businesses all look for capable and efficient people, and often, companies open up new positions to accommodate valuable employees. Anyone looking for a job has to convince the business owner that their contribution within the company can enhance its prosperity and growth. To be convincing, job seekers must identify precisely what kind of person is best suited to do the job on hand. Unfortunately, most people come to interviews unprepared; they simply describe their idea of the perfect job.

Today, given the expenses related to each job in an organization, small work teams are the preference. Instead of hiring new people, companies encourage overtime. Individuals who want a place on the job market must convince prospective employers that hiring them would be a positive decision.

Paving the Way

Before bringing up a difficult topic or sharing a criticism, I pave the way. I treasure my relationship with the other person, which means that before bringing up a difficult topic, I tell him or her how important our relationship is to me. Then I take the time to explain why I want to bring up this particular subject and I remember that I must accept the fact that I may be given a very direct answer. By preparing the ground that good communication requires, I can achieve my goals and strengthen my relationships.

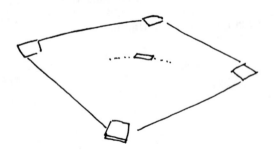

Going Beyond Limitations

"We are all here to go beyond our initial limitations, regardless of what they are. We are here to recognize our magnificent and divine nature, regardless of what it tells us."

— LOUISE HAY

A barrier is an obstacle that prevents us from achieving a goal or that stops our growth. Life involves all sorts of barriers. But the most challenging barriers are those that we impose upon ourselves. These barriers are hard to overcome because we cannot see them. They are so much a part of our way of thinking and seeing things that they are invisible to us. Throughout our path to self-fulfillment, we must examine the attitudes, perceptions and behaviors that hinder our progress. It is only when we can clearly identify our personal barriers that we can find the road that leads to serenity.

The Ideal Scenario

"You have to accept life as it comes, but you should try to make sure that it comes just the way you'd like it."

— GERMAN SAYING

The ideal scenario is the life I want to create for myself, the ideal life as I imagine it. When my ideal scenario is about to come true, I recognize it because I've already imagined it in detail. And when I begin to move away from it I can remedy the situation. I turn to my imagination and look at my ideal scenario again. It doesn't matter what my focus is: money, my love relationship, my family, my career. By imagining my ideal scenario, I create a clear vision of the future and I see myself moving forward.

I can strive with all my heart to achieve what I see in my imagination. I can develop my vision of the future. I can develop a clear vision of the life I want to lead. I can achieve this objective because I can set aside the people and things that prevent me from making my ideal scenario come true.

My Plan of Attack

"You may have habits that weaken you. The secret to change is focusing your energy not on fighting against the past, but on building the future."
— SOCRATES

Today, I am interested in planning. I have understood that to make progress, I must set objectives and I must give myself the means of achieving them. I am completely responsible for my life and the path I travel on this earth. I know what is good for me and for those I love.

Today, I will draw up a plan of attack to achieve the objectives that are important to me.

① ——————

② ——————

③ ——————

④ ——————

⑤ ——————

⑥ ——————

My Hopes

Today, I remember my hopes. For a long time, I stopped hoping that I could achieve my goals and make my fondest dreams come true. At times I was discouraged, the obstacles in my path seemed insurmountable and gradually, I lost my wings. But the strength within me, greater than life itself, brought my dreams back to me.

Surveys

Today, I see how important it is to be aware of my customers' expectations and requirements so I conduct surveys on a regular basis. Of course, I can use the standard survey method: a well structured questionnaire. But I can also conduct ongoing surveys by asking the people around me and the people who do business with me to share their opinions. I've always been interested in what people think of my products and services and how they react to them. Their impressions nurture and guide my efforts. I want to know as much as I can about what people think of my products or services and I want to adapt them to meet customer needs.

Today, I show interest in the opinions and the viewpoints of others. I want to know them, so I ask the right questions and I stay calm and objective with regard to the reactions I get.

Seeing Beyond the Surface

Appearances can be deceiving. A failure may be a victory if you know how to learn from it. A rejection may be an opportunity to move on to something else. The end of one relationship marks the start of a new one. Change is omnipresent in our lives. We should never cling to any one situation. Instead, in the end of an experience, we should see the beginning of something new.

When I embrace the natural cycle of birth, growth, decline and death, I do not see death as an end, I see it as a beginning. Once the darkness has eliminated the last light of dusk, not long after, it must give way to the first glimmer of dawn. I need not fear the darkness for it contains the seeds of light.

Choosing or Not Choosing

We are constantly asked to give, to participate, to buy and to sell. We should keep in mind that we have our own projects, our own objectives, our own ambitions. We are completely free to choose whether or not we want to participate.

I can say yes, I can say no, I can say maybe, or I can say that I can't decide right now. I have a whole range of possibilities to choose from. And I keep in mind that I have my own priorities.

Today, I know that I am free to choose and I am equally free not to choose.

Sobriety

Sobriety and personal success go hand in hand. How can we imagine it possible to reach our full potential if we are struggling with the problem of addictions? How can we be happy and how can we live in harmony with others if we are dependent and if our senses and emotions are in turmoil? How can we achieve our objectives if our faculties are affected?

Today, I resolve to live a sober and well-balanced life. Today, I choose to live in full possession of my faculties and with my eyes opened wide to what is happening around me. I know that my accomplishments bring me joy and personal satisfaction. I know that if I want to succeed, I must see things clearly and I must be calm and composed.

Each Minute is a New Minute

Today, I know that each minute brings with it new possibilities, a new window on the world around me. Each minute of my life, I can see the beauty around me and I can do my share to make it even more beautiful.

Today, I know that I can undergo renewal every minute. I rejoice in the fact that every single thing changes. Every thing undergoes constant transformation. I will not resist the process of renewal and change. I will let the flow of renewal and change sweep me toward endless new possibilities.

The Retailer's Vision

The consumer's viewpoint is different from the manufacturer's viewpoint. The retailer sees things in a way that is different from the distributor's. The distributor's concerns are different from the retailer's. But despite these divergent viewpoints, the capitalist system works, and each group's interests are protected. Commerce is based on a series of practical compromises that lead to a response to a need or a requirement. Retailers must be objective since they must deal with the consumer's right to buy or not to buy. The retailer's mission is to work from the viewpoint of the consumer as well as all the other groups involved in the manufacturing and distribution process.

This wonderful ability to look at things from the viewpoint and reality of others is what gives the retailer the freedom of action that leads to success.

The Principle of Non-action

There is an ancient book of wisdom written by a Chinese philosopher named Lao Tzu ("Old Master"). The book was written several thousand years ago and it talks about the road to peace and serenity. In his book, the *Tao-ti-Chin*, Lao Tzu outlines the virtues of non-action. Non-action means the ability to wait, to observe, to listen and to explore before acting. Each event is driven by its own dynamics in relation to the laws of the universe. At times, the biggest mistake we can make is taking action instead of letting things take their course. The impatient individual is unable to take the time to explore; he rushes headlong into action and as a result, upsets the natural order of things. There is an important message here. Action must be in harmony with the situation and, at times, not taking action and letting events take their course is the best decision.

Consensus

"At poker, you have to be able to win with a losing hand and lose with a winning hand."
— THE FILM "HAVANA"

The dynamics of poker are much like the dynamics of life itself. If you bet only on winning hands, you spend your time waiting for fate to deal you the ideal hand. But a good player can bet and win with a very weak hand if he manages to convince his opponents that he has a winning hand.

Our success results from our ability to convince others that we're winners. We have to win over people if we want to reach our objectives. Winning others over to our side involves no trickery. All it takes is confidence in our own ability to create a consensus on the value of a given project. When the consensus is that the project will be successful, then it will be successful.

Persistence

Today, I know that no one can deny the importance of persistence and the contribution it makes to success. A persistent person is true and strong and worthy of recognition. A persistent person finds a place in the world. A persistent person has a lasting effect on those around him or her.

I see that in spite of difficulties and hardships, I will persist. And in the long run, my persistence will be rewarded by recognition and respect. We forget things that are ephemeral, but what persists is always part of our lives.

Today, I choose to persist.

Major Victories

On the road to success, there are small daily victories and major victories. Major victories include being able to expand a business within a short period of time, offering a wide range of products and increasing profits to a level well beyond mere survival. A major victory comes when we see an important change in the nature of the company and its activities. For example, when the offices occupied for the past five years no longer provide enough space given increases in production capacity; or when, after several years of careful investment, as owners, we can finally be rewarded with a good salary without jeopardizing the enterprise; when we can take a three-week vacation and the company runs smoothly. Major victories are proof that we have reached another stage in development.

Today, I lay the groundwork for major victories. I resolve to increase my production and improve my service. I resolve to find new clients while remembering to strengthen my relationship with current clients.

The Wealth of Maturity

"Today, I have a positive outlook on old age and the wealth it brings. Just as I used to cherish the wealth of the child within me, I value the things that growing old will bring me as I advance in age."

— ROKELLE LERNER

Physical bodies age. I cannot escape this truth. But I am a being who stays young, open-minded and energetic. I pay very little attention to the phenomenon of ageing. I concentrate my attention and my energy on my true nature and on my true worth as a human being.

Personal success depends not on age, but on enthusiasm and resolve. I refuse to abandon my projects or to let my ambitions fade away simply because I am growing old. On the contrary, I will use the wisdom and experience that growing old brings to guide me in my life journey.

My Fundamental Wisdom

One truth is very well masked by the appearance of things and by the current structure of modern societies which attach more importance to things and to the body while minimizing the importance of the spiritual being: the ultimate value and importance of our fundamental wisdom and our spiritual life.

Throughout our lives, we receive advice, truths and ideas of all sorts. I listen to others, but I know that I must listen to my own wisdom and to my own ideals as well. The more I develop the ability to listen to myself, the more faithful I will be to myself and the more in harmony I will be with my innate wisdom.

Today, I listen to my own wisdom. And by listening to my inner self, I encourage the development of my spiritual life.

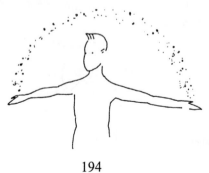

Serving Others

"Life teaches us that the only worthwhile endeavor is serving others."

— LEWIS CARROLL

Today, I choose to serve others. I see that life is fuller and richer when I give of myself and when I am open to serving others. I am not here for myself alone, I am here to contribute to the happiness of others. When I help someone, I fulfill my divine mission. When I serve someone, I advance on the road to happiness and serenity.

Success is based on sharing and exchange. When I give generously, I know that I open the door to abundance in my own life. If I hold back and am reluctant to give, I create a sterile environment in which no life, no love and no exchange can manifest itself. When I give willingly, all of life's possibilities are available to me.

Negotiation

"To get to the promised land, each of us must negotiate a road through the jungle."
— HERB COHEN

Between my dreams and their achievement lies a whole world. A world filled with solutions, stumbling blocks, resources, barriers and many other factors that will come into play in the material achievement of my dream. We live in a world of constant change and each day, we should look for the advantages it brings us. I am a spiritual being living in a material world. I must deal with my inner self, my dreams and my true nature and I must deal with other human beings and the world of material things. I must cling to my ideas and to the achievement of my dreams. Not an easy feat!

Knowing that everything can be negotiated, I believe in the principle that I can reach my objectives through communication, the ability to find solutions that are mutually satisfactory to all involved, and by asking for the help of others when I need it. Negotiation is not compromise. Negotiation is the act of including others in my search for achievement. Negotiation is the art of serving others while I reach my own goals.

A Moment Can Change a Life

"There are people who leave a mark on our lives, even if for only one moment. And after that moment, we are never the same. Time has no importance, but certain moments are important forever."

— FERN BORK

As I look back on my life, I realize that certain decisions, certain encounters, certain meetings and certain events were extremely determinant in my personal growth. These crucial moments profoundly changed the course of my life. A few moments to change an entire life! A few minutes to change me forever! Such moments are precious and rare. They happen because of universal laws or because we have intentionally created them for ourselves. They stand at crossroads in our lives. Today or tomorrow, one of these wonderful moments may occur in my life. And I will be faced with an important decision that will mark my existence until the end of my days.

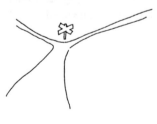

Confronting Our Fears

"Robert Frost said: 'The best way to get out of a bad situation is to go through it.' This is all the more true when the situation involves our fears. In reality, the only way to escape our fears is to confront them. When we run from our fears, they catch up with us. Fears we fail to face cloud our vision and hide from us the infinite possibilities available to us. Fear is also a magnet that attracts to us exactly what we fear."

— SUE PATTON THOELE

Here I am, here and now, with my past: my experiences, my fears, my desires, my "I should have's" and my "I could have's", my strengths and my weaknesses. Ahead of me, I know that there are other life experiences, things to accomplish, things to see.

Today, I take myself by the hand and I move forward. Yes, I have experienced hardships, failures and problems. But now, I am wiser and I resolve to continue to live and grow. I have courage and I can travel the road ahead of me.

Criticism

"Instead of condemning people, we should try to understand them. We should try to understand why they do the things they do. Understanding is much more positive and profitable than criticism and it generates much more sympathy, tolerance and benevolence."

— DALE CARNEGIE

In every day life, I encounter many unexpected situations. I often wonder about people's motivations and behaviors. Sometimes, someone around me does something that truly upsets me, that shatters my ability to be efficient and that seems to stop me from reaching my objectives. Although on the inside I may react angrily or emotionally, I always take time out before I discuss the issue with that person. I know that harsh criticism leads nowhere.

I have realized that most of the time, the person who has hurt me thought that he or she was doing nothing wrong. Through dialogue and exchange, we can build lasting ties of mutual help. The criticism that stems from anger and emotion is always much less efficient and effective than constructive dialogue can be.

Recognizing Our Excellence

"People who are critical all the time see their mistakes through a magnifying glass and their successes as small objects in the background. They use a telescope to look at their real and imagined weaknesses, and then turn it around and use the opposite end to look at their qualities and their successes. Mistakes look huge and successes look microscopic."

— SUE PATTON THOELE

Today, I congratulate myself on my successes, big or small. I refuse to focus on the mistakes I have made and I take the time to see that overall, I have experienced many more successes than failures. I do good work each day and I am an efficient person. I congratulate myself on my efficiency and I recognize my own excellence.

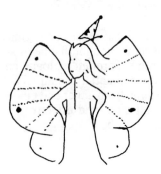

The Qualities of a Leader

What are the qualities of a leader? According to Napoleon Hill, a noted author, a leader has the following qualities: he is courageous, he has self-control, he is fair, he is decisive, he is generous, he is likeable, he pays attention to details, he shoulders his responsibilities at all times and he is cooperative.

A leader has initiative. He organizes new projects and proposes new solutions. A leader is a man or woman of action, someone who is not afraid to take calculated risks. A leader does not need the approval of others before taking on a new project; he knows how to find a consensus and draw up a good plan of action based on that consensus. He surrounds himself with reliable and competent individuals and he knows how to sustain their enthusiasm. A leader is a warrior, trained in the art and strategy of warfare. He is a skilled negotiator and he knows that everything can be negotiated successfully and that negotiating makes everyone a winner, no matter what the situation.

The Power of Convictions

Personal success requires a form of stubbornness. We must believe firmly in the principles and values that guide our decisions and our growth. We must be firmly convinced that the path we've chosen is the right one for us. We must resist the temptation to give up when we encounter obstacles or stumbling blocks along our way. We must be completely and absolutely convinced that we are right.

Today, I have the power of my convictions. I am unwavering and I am sure of myself. I believe in the mission I have taken on and I refuse to be distracted or confused by outside forces. Yes, the power of my convictions brings with it the creativity and the ability to take on challenges of any kind. Yes, the power of my convictions brings with it a long road that I must travel to reach self-fulfillment and personal success.

A Winner's Attitude

"Success is not something you find at the end of the road. You find it as you travel, all along your road."

— FRANÇOIS GARAGNON

Today, I resolve to adopt a winner's attitude. I set out with the knowledge that I will succeed. Each obstacle and each barrier on my road can be used to make me stronger. I deserve to succeed and I set out with the desire to embrace life.

Today, I belong to myself!

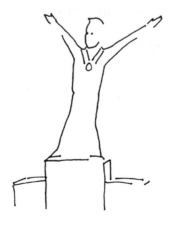

Imagine

"What man can imagine and what he can believe in, he can achieve."

— NAPOLEON HILL

Action is not a guarantee of success. There is an ideal backdrop to success. Success starts in our minds and in our attitudes. I use my imagination. I use my ability to dream to feed and inspire my action. Each day, I have new ideas, new strategies, new plans for moving forward, ever closer to my objectives for growth and self-fulfillment. Most of my ideas will never materialize. But some will lift me higher and bring me further.

I test my ideas in the material world, sometimes by asking questions, sometimes by taking action. I know that my imagination leads me to success because it lets me invent and create.

Today, I give free reign to my imagination because I know that it is the secret to my success.

Feeling Good

"People who feel good get the best results".
— K. BLANCHARD AND S. JOHNSON

Today, I know that I get the best results when I feel good. To feel good, I have to eat well, exercise regularly, get enough rest and take the time to enjoy myself. I must also know how to reward myself for a good day's work. I must recognize and underline my accomplishments.

When someone compliments me, I accept the compliment. Yes, I am a person who is worthy of love and appreciation. Yes, I am a very valuable person. Yes, when I resolve to do the right things in all my relationships and interactions with others, I feel good.

Looking at Your Performance

"Take a minute: look at your objectives. Look at your performance. Determine whether your behavior reflects your objectives."
— K. BLANCHARD AND S. JOHNSON

I have realized that setting objectives isn't enough. I have to go further. I have to imagine how things will be once I have reached my objectives. Then I have to evaluate my performance in light of my objectives. If I do this or that, will it bring me closer or farther from my objectives? Am I efficient? How can I move ahead faster and more effectively on the road that leads to my goals? I have to set up a system to measure my performance against my objectives and I have to use my system every day. When I do, it lets me do what I have to do to make sure that I stay exactly on course.

The Power of Appreciation

*"Help people reach their full potential. Give them
the experience of doing something well."*
— K. BLANCHARD AND S. JOHNSON

I keep in mind that to be a good manager, I have
to work well with others. I have to encourage and
sustain cooperation among the members of my
team. People work for more than a salary. They
work for self-fulfillment. They work to achieve
their full potential. I want to be a good manager
and I want to help others achieve their own goals.
So I encourage them and I compliment them for
work well done. Everyone wants to hear that
they've done something well. Everyone wants to
be recognized and appreciated.

Today, I take the time to tell the people who work
with me how much I appreciate their cooperation
and their presence.

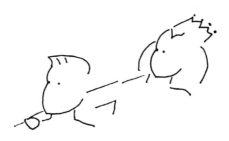

Seeing Through Other People's Eyes

"The biggest secret to success is the ability to see things through the other person's eyes and to look at things from a different angle than your own point of view."

— HENRY FORD

Each person has their own preoccupations and their own desires. If to serve my own purposes I insist on trying to persuade other people they should see things my way, I will be bitterly disappointed. I must develop the ability to see what other people want and to look at things as they see them. I will win their support if I can help them reach their own objectives.

Today, I know that if I want to sell a product or a service to someone, I must have the ability to fulfill their needs and to meet their expectations. I must listen carefully to their objections and their concerns if I want to be persuasive.

Reclaiming Excellence

"We often have a hard time getting past the mistaken ideas we have about ourselves — to the point that we can't even see our own excellence."
— SUE PATTON THOELE

People who are committed to excellence never lack work. Clients seek them out because they are dedicated to their work and because they deliver a product or a service of consistently good quality. When I am committed to excellence, I bring a new intensity to my work and I achieve a higher level of service.

Today, I have decided that excellence is my personal minimum requirement. I am completely committed to my work and I refuse to compromise on the quality of my product. I choose excellence because when I do, I make the best use of the most precious aspects of my inner self.

A Decision Can Change Everything

"Succeeding is being deeply and completely convinced that we have the ability to succeed. External factors are unimportant compared to the unrelenting power inside of us."
— FRANÇOIS GARAGNON

I know that a single decision can change everything. From the moment we decide to live a new kind of life, to base our lives and our growth on new principles, everything can change. Success does not depend on the environment I live in or on the material conditions of my existence; instead, it depends on my strength of character and my persistence. From the moment I decide to end my suffering, financial dependence or uncertainty, everything changes.

Of course, if our basic commitment is to stay powerless and to live blindly instead of affirming our beliefs, a spontaneous decision will change nothing. But if we are truly determined to achieve our goals, absolutely no one can stop us.

Today, I resolve that I can have exactly the kind of life I want.

Taxes

Today, people complain that they pay too much tax. And at times it seems as if the national pastime is trying to pay as little tax as possible. Most people would agree that there is a problem and that the current level of taxation discourages work, job creation and investment. I make peace with the issue of taxes in two ways: 1) I use an honest and efficient account that helps me plan my taxes, and 2) I pay my taxes religiously. This way I can focus my energy on production and developing my business activities and I can sleep in peace.

Today, I accept the fact that there is a social cost related to business. That cost is an undeniable reality. I want to be worry-free and so I play according to the rules of the game.

Feeling Successful

The feeling I associate most closely with success is pride. The pride of doing a good day's work. The pride of creating something beautiful or something new. The pride of belonging to an excellent team. The pride of being a good parent. The pride of achieving positive results. The pride of developing good relationships. For me, pride shows that I have something positive that can contribute not only to my happiness, but to the happiness of others.

Today, I am proud to be me. I am proud of the person I am and of the person I am becoming. I am proud of all my small and major accomplishments. I am proud to be a good citizen, a good parent and a good child. I am proud to be a good friend and of speaking openly about my love for you.

Business Women

Generally speaking, the business world resisted the advent of women into its ranks. Resistance came from many fronts: banking system, governments, suppliers, employers. But we've made great strides in the last ten years. Now we see that businesses managed by women are generally managed more efficiently and more profitably than those run by men. Women deserve their place in the business world because they are capable of great dedication. They believe in quality and they believe in sound and effective management. They can work and succeed under difficult circumstances because they refuse to give in. They refuse to accept defeat and they are ready to make the compromises needed to ensure their business' survival. They also have an extraordinary sense of responsibility, sharing and collective effort.

We must encourage women to start their own businesses and we must encourage their expansion. The presence of women in the business world raises it to a higher level of ethics and contributes to the great good of society as a whole.

Family Life

When you look at the question of personal success, it is impossible to ignore family life. Our families have undergone enormous changes in the last two decades. Today, we often live through the effects of the breakdown of the family unit. However, the family remains a source of joy, of security, of belonging and emotional stability. Within the family, we learn to share, to love, to take our individual responsibilities and to take pleasure in the company of others.

Today, I see that family life is part of my sense of values. I seek to reinforce and nurture my ties with other family members. I am willing to help them, comfort them and spoil them. I know that alone, life makes no real sense. So I seek to create sound, loving and lasting ties with my family.

There's Always a Solution

We should return to a simpler approach to life. In a sense, we should return to our roots. When we try to complicate life, we experience problems. If I have a disagreement with a colleague or a friend, I wait for my anger to dissipate and I go to him or her to explain my point of view frankly, and I am prepared to admit that I may have been wrong in some ways. If my children come home with a bad report card, I spend more time with them to help them understand the things they find hard to learn. If colleagues or acquaintances react coldly to me, I seek them out and I ask them to explain what's wrong. In short, there is always a way to make life simpler.

Taking a Break

Sometimes, I need a longer break. So since I like sports, I go for a run, play a little tennis or do any other kind of exercise that will get me away from my routine work activities and help me forget the things that may be worrying me. Very often, when I come back from this kind of escapade, things seem clearer and as if by magic, solutions begin to come to mind. There are probably a thousand and one ways to make our lives easier and simpler. Everyone should consider how their lives could be better, and then find ways to carry out their strategies. And we should also reevaluate our regular routines, keeping the positive and finding solutions for the negative.

Appearances Can be Deceiving

Our consumer-based societies encourage us to buy, buy, buy. They would have us believe that happiness and success increase with the purchase and ownership of goods. Our houses, our apartments and our businesses are filled with all sorts of consumer goods that in fact, contribute nothing to our happiness or to our success. The credit purchase system only makes us more vulnerable to financial problems of various kinds. I am moving farther and farther away from the notion that I must demonstrate my success by giving the appearance that I am rich and happy. I am an increasingly wise and practical consumer who limits purchases to what is truly needed.

I am not a miser. I am simply a part of the group of people who are increasingly aware that materialism is a thing of the past and that overconsumption hurts the quality of life we enjoy. My focus is my relationships with people. I take pleasure in working and creating. For me, success is synonymous with freedom of choice and self-reliance.

Using the Telephone

Modern telephony is flourishing. And with it, so has our hard-earned money. Today, I realize that the telephone is a work tool. I keep a close watch on my consumption of telephone services because I know that my money goes fast when I indulge in idle talk on the telephone. Special deals to cut the cost of long-distance or international calls, cell phone, call waiting, directory assistance and chat lines all contribute — without exception — to increasing our expenses without increasing our satisfaction or our efficiency.

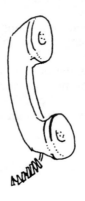

The Wealthy Person's Profile

I believe that you need not be cheap to become wealthy. Rich people seem to share certain characteristics: they ask the right questions, they are usually patient and they know how to wait for the right opportunity; before taking a step, they gather as much information as they can; they know how to work intelligently; they know how to save and build a reserve fund.

Why dream of getting rich quick through some special circumstance? I can behave in such a way as to maximize my efforts. I can ask the right questions. I can be patient and I can take action when the right opportunity comes along. I work hard and I have the self-discipline to save. I can develop the reflexes and the behaviors that help me accumulate wealth.

Success isn't an Accident

Economists, bankers and accountants all have something in common. They usually know how to recognize a good business opportunity. By analyzing the numbers, they can see that a business is turning a profit and is prospering from one year to another. Such prosperity is never accidental. It is the result of a conscious effort and of specific actions designed to increase sales and to achieve a profit situation.

Everyone who wants to succeed in business must develop a basic knowledge of the factors that contribute to the growth and sound management of businesses. There are principles and means of analysis that ensure the survival and growth of companies. In business, intuition is good as well, but only to a certain point. Beyond that point, developing a system for analyzing statistics, keeping a close watch on profit margins and applying ratios is crucial. All these mechanisms will help us achieve our goals.

Growth

Today, I know that growth is the most wonderful of all games. I established a small business and then, I worked to make it grow. I quickly realized that I had to analyze my progress, so I set up a system for analyzing statistics. I analyze the increases and decreases in my sales figures. I constantly look for ways to expand my business, to serve my clients more efficiently, to offer the best possible services, to improve my production and my product. When I do something that results in an increase in sales, I maintain my strategy and I expand on it. When I do something that results in a drop in sales, I look for a different strategy.

Today, I see that analyzing statistics is crucial to my success. How can I trace my progress if I fail to analyze the statistics which apply to my situation and to my productivity?

Finding Solutions

Today, I know that there is a solution to every problem. Most of the time, by standing back, talking and briefly analyzing the situations, I can find the right solution. At other times, I am confronted with a major problem that may be a serious threat to the proper functioning of my company. I have decided that I like major problems because they lead me to grow and to use my full potential. Major problems are a test and they invite me to go beyond my limitations and my usual considerations.

Today, I embrace problems because I know that there is always a solution. I see problems as a positive activity because I know that this way, I can make the best of my full potential, my imagination and my creativity. Ultimately, I know that I am bigger than any problem I may encounter.

The Greatest Reward

"Tell people how good you feel when they do their work well and how much their work means to the organization and to their colleagues."
— K. BLANCHARD AND S. JOHNSON

Things are easy to take for granted. Businesses offer a salary and fringe benefit and everyone seems to think that's all a job involves. But for an employee, the greatest reward isn't a salary, fringe benefits or the prestige he or she may get from working for a given company. An employee's greatest reward is the appreciation of colleagues and superiors. The most important thing most of us neglect to do is to express aloud and sincerely how much we appreciate our employees or our colleagues.

Today, I take the time to give compliments, to express my appreciation and to encourage my colleagues, my employees and my suppliers.

Flying High

"We have the choice between flying high, in an atmosphere of optimism, enthusiasm and energy, or spending our time depressed and stuck on the ground. Do the attitudes we adopt reflect the pure air of the higher reaches of the atmosphere, or are they polluted by the air you find at ground level? Each of us is free to adopt our own vision of things. If we don't like what we see, we have the courage and the ability to change things."
— SUE PATTON THOELE

When an individual listens to his superior being, he reaches a higher level of knowledge and awareness. He drinks at the well of discernment, a faculty which belongs to the subtle world of the spirit. He can come to know the world by looking beyond appearances and by targeting loftier goals. The superior being always triumphs because he is based on the virtues of the heart — kindness, goodness, compassion — and he can achieve his goals with the blessing of the universe.

Today, I choose to take the high road. I use my discernment and my compassion as well as my commitment to excellence to guide me and to help me move forward and grow.

Choosing the Right Path

Each person can find a professional activity that suits them. Each person has the talents and the abilities needed to play a useful role within the working world and within society. Each person has his or her own special place and each has the right to take that place with the goal of making society a better place for all.

Today, I recognize that I too have the right to take my place in society. I deserve to take my place among those who are successful and who contribute, through their activities, to the well-being and growth of the community. I am a full-fledged member of society and I have a right to work, to dignity and to prosperity.

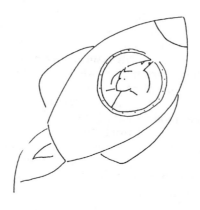

Moderation in All

"Perfect reason avoids extremes and seeks the wisdom of sobriety."

— MOLIÈRE

It is difficult to discuss temperance without sounding preachy. Yet those who suffer in the present because of their excesses in the past have only themselves to blame. It is so easy to overindulge in good things, we can easily become trapped without even realizing that we are. In such instances, we are the victims of our own negative behavior patterns. Temperance is a virtue that serves as an alarm as soon as we fall into excess.

In our modern era, temperance is a virtue that has been almost completely set aside. The revolutionary ideas of the sixties swept away all restraint and encouraged many different types of excesses. But gradually, we are returning to sounder values, including temperance. More and more people realize that we can enjoy the pleasures of life much more fully and much longer when we practice moderation. Major efforts have been made on several fronts to educate and convince the population. And this can only be in the best interests of everyone. The rewards of moderation are good health, a better quality of life and personal success.

Mutual Respect

Competition can be very healthy. When we have competitors, we are continually forced to do our best and to look for ways to improve our product or service so that we can keep our place in the market and continue to expand. In itself, competition is healthy and it benefits everyone involved, including the consumer. We have all seen that the absence of competition in Eastern European countries resulted in bankruptcies, inferior quality products, general poverty and a total breakdown of the system. Those who fight to limit competition in the marketplace have a completely faulty outlook on its impact.

Today, I see that success must be based on competition and the respect of competitors. When I respect my competitors, I remain watchful and active. I refuse to rest on my laurels. I analyze the actions and the products of my competitors and I try to find ways in which to improve my own business.

We Can't Avoid All Conflicts

Today, I know that it isn't always possible to avoid conflict. At times, my interests or my intentions are in conflict with the interests or intentions of others. I know that most conflicts can be settled positively through dialogue and negotiation. I no longer avoid conflict, but nor do I look for it. When I see that a decision is likely to result in very negative reactions, I try to find a new approach.

There is no need to live in a climate of conflict and disagreement. I can avoid most conflicts by foreseeing reactions and by being flexible. Today, I know how to grow and move ahead without causing needless conflicts. When a conflict does occur, I am flexible enough to find a winning solution that lets me continue on my path to success.

Knowing What is Important

Schools don't necessarily teach us that we should show an interest in others. However, our sincere interest in others can often be a determining factor. Each of us is preoccupied with our own lives and mostly aware of our own needs. If I want to succeed, I must show an interest in others. I must look at situations from their point of view. I must demonstrate that I am sincerely interested in others, in their needs and in the satisfaction of their needs.

When I meet new people, I deepen my relationship with them by asking them how they are. I show that I am interested in their current situations, in their families, in their quality of life. I show an interest in other people and I try to understand them.

Permission to Enjoy Myself

How can I achieve a higher level of well-being if I fail to enjoy life? Personal success includes the ability to relax, to have fun and to laugh. If my everyday life is a chore and if I live in the hopes of becoming rich one day so that I can finally start to enjoy life, I've already missed the boat. For me, success is synonymous with joy, pleasure and passion. So I seek to enjoy life every single day. I give myself permission to enjoy life.

Today, I look around me and I see the things that bring me joy. I plan activities that I know I will enjoy. I take the time to meet with my friends and I give myself permission to laugh and to have fun with them.

Today, I Feel Powerful

Today, I feel powerful. I am the master of my own destiny. I can create positive and lasting effects in my life. I can take action. I see my objectives clearly and I am aware of my commitment to move forward. There is a powerful force burning inside me and pushing me forward. This day belongs to me. I am capable of seeing the opportunities it brings me. I am aware. I live in the present moment. I am powerful.

Motivation

Everybody talks about motivation, but what exactly is it? There are motivational courses, motivational seminars and books on motivation. Psychologists refer to motivation time and time again, but they fail to motivate anyone. Motivated individuals are rarely interested in motivation because they are already motivated. They are active, powered by their dreams and their commitment to getting things done.

When we try to motivate ourselves just to get through the day, we've already missed the boat of motivation.

Today, I no longer wonder about motivation. Instead, I take action. I look straight ahead and I travel toward my goal. I no longer look to see if outside circumstances are favorable or not before I take action. No one else need tell me what to do. I am motivated.

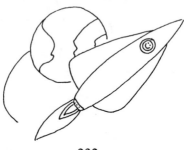

Wiping the Slate Clean

Everyday life is filled with examples of people who harbor a resentment against a colleague, an acquaintance or a family member. The resentment can last for days, months, even years. Most of us have encountered someone who, choking back tears, tells the story of how sorry they feel that someone in their lives died before there could be forgiveness between the two of them. This type of testimonial is upsetting and no one should have to experience such a situation.

There are various religious days or events during which the faithful forgive those who have offended them in some way. Two examples are the pilgrimage to St. Anne d'Auray in Brittany or the Day of Atonement in the Jewish faith. I know a family that gathers each evening after supper for a time of prayer. And before the other members of the family and even before guests, each must ask forgiveness for all they have done that may have offended or hurt someone else. At times this leads to lively discussions, but the meeting always ends peacefully. For this particular family, this is a way to practise the principle: *"Forgive us our trespasses, as we forgive those who trespass against us."*

I Control My Life

Success requires a fair amount of personal discipline and control. I know that I won't be able to do the things I like every single day. I work to achieve my goals and I must handle the variety of tasks that they involve. Sometimes, I'd like to be able to drop everything and just do nothing. At this point, personal discipline is vital to my success. I am capable of self-control and I can make a consistent effort. I accept the responsibility to work hard at my projects even when this means overtime or missing a spontaneous outing.

Discipline and self-control make me feel content because I know that I can rely on myself to get my projects done. I am motivated by my objectives and my ideals, not by the need for instant gratification.

Today, I resolve to be disciplined in my work. When I show discipline, I control my life and my destiny. I say no to all the outside temptations that urge me to set aside my work and I follow my path to personal success.

The Art of War

War is certainly not a constructive activity. But many war strategies are used in the business world. We associate our competitors with our enemies and we seek to invade their territory by formulating offensive strategies. And when our own territory is threatened by our competitors, we apply defensive strategies to protect our assets. Many war tactics and strategies are found in the business world. Ultimately, we must be on the alert and we must be able to fend for ourselves if we want to survive in the fiercely competitive climate that prevails in the business world.

Today, I am watchful and aware. I observe the movements and the behaviors of my competitors. I use offensive strategies to carve out a place in the market. When my position is threatened, I react quickly to eliminate danger.

Reinvesting Profits

A business' success is based on the ability to generate profits and, more importantly, the reinvestment of profits to ensure sustained growth. If all of a company's surplus income is used for personal ends, the company is doomed to stagnate. Naturally, each of us wants to be rewarded for our efforts, but at the same time, it is important to expand our businesses and to develop their production capacities. In the first few years and throughout a business' existence, a major percentage of profits must be reinvested for the purchase of equipment, the hiring of new employees or the development of new product lines.

Today, I see my business as a living and independent being. I nurture its growth by reinvesting part of my profits in it. In this way, I am a good manager and I am ensuring my future prosperity.

I Deserve a Vacation

When I am very heavily involved in achieving my objectives, I can forget my own needs. A vacation — or a least a few weeks outside the home or the office — help us recharge our batteries. When I leave on a vacation, to some extent I get away from day-to-day concerns and the imperatives of work. During a vacation, my only priorities are enjoying myself, resting and relaxing. Yes, I have worked hard and I deserve a vacation. Yes, I can get away for a while and I can think only of myself.

Today, I see that vacations are essential to my morale and to my physical and mental well-being. If I work without ever taking a break, I am less productive.

Through the Eyes of a Child

"For me, true adults are not those with over-whelming 'maturity', but those who have kept a child's innocence. They have sparks in their eyes and a child's spring in their step."

— JUDY FORD

Are you like me in the springtime, when the snow begins to melt and the sun's rays begin to feel warmer? I work with a great deal of caring and love at what will soon be a magnificent flower garden. I take pleasure in imagining the colors and scents that I will enjoy in my garden as I sow tiny, fragile seeds.

That's how I imagine the children of this world, mine and those of others. They are small seeds asking only to sprout, grow in beauty and bring their contribution to building this world. As a parent, I have the responsibility of helping them grow in an atmosphere of respect and harmony. I always keep in mind that they will probably be parents themselves one day and that they will raise their own children. I am and I will always be a model for them.

Personal Problems at Work

When I entered the job market, people often used to mention that personal problems had no place in the work world. At the time, I thought that this meant that no one should arrive at work looking worried or depressed. With time, I realized that the notion went further. Today, I see that the work place is designed as a place that can sustain stable production levels. Contact with clients and suppliers and between team members should be open and courteous. I must be in a state of mind that lets me respond efficiently to the needs of those around me and to take on my responsibilities within an organization. Therefore, I must have enough strength of character to put my own personal preoccupations aside.

Today, I understand that I must be in a position to fulfill my responsibilities. When I come to the office, I set aside my moods and my preoccupations and I focus my attention on the tasks at hand. Often, as I work, the small things that had been affecting me disappear and I feel happy again.

Knowing How to Delegate

Today, I see that my business' growth will be determined by my ability to delegate. When people set up a small business, they tend to want to do everything themselves. In the beginning, this reflex is very valuable because it gives them control over all aspects of the operation. But as the business grows, I must learn to give some responsibility to others. If I do not have the ability to delegate, my business' growth will be slowed and limited by the things that I leave undone in the course of a day.

Today, I realize that it is important to delegate. I give others the responsibility of carrying out various tasks and taking charge of various business activities. I work with them and I encourage them. Gradually, I hand over some of my responsibilities and I adopt a principle of sound management. I set performance objectives for my colleagues and I reward work that is well done. Today, more and more, I delegate and I can see my business grow.

Personnel Training

There can be no doubt that personnel training is the biggest investment that today's companies make. From the time new employees come through the door, they represent a major salary expense and during the first few months, they work below their full performance potential. But the value inherent in the service or product the company offers is generated by employees. This is why human resources are the most valuable of all company's resources.

Today, I am aware of the value of the people who work for me. I take the time to choose with care the people who will be part of my team and then I devote the time and energy needed to train them well. I see that with time, a new member of the team will take my place and will contribute to increasing the company's worth.

Today, I Ask What I Can Do for You

"Ask not what your country can do for you. Ask what you can do for your country."
— JOHN F. KENNEDY

Anyone who wants to succeed should ask themselves the following questions: what are my customers' needs and how can I satisfy them? It's easy to see how useful this formula can be when we are looking for a job, developing our customer base, opening new markets or increasing our sales. Instead of focusing on our own needs, we focus our attention on the needs of others. By doing so, we find new solutions to old problems, we develop new products and new services, but most importantly, we carve out a permanent place among our customers by becoming indispensable.

Today, instead of focusing on my own needs, I seek to fill the needs of others and to meet their expectations. In this way, I become indispensable and I am rewarded for my efforts.

Tangible Proof of My Success

"When I set out to make my first million, no one wanted to help me. Now that I am working on my second million, everybody wants to help me."
— RICHARD PAQUETTE

There are many things that serve as proof of success: an increase in our revenues; an increase in the number of clients we have; an increase in sales; an increase in the quality and the quantity of our products or our services; quick and easier access to various sources of financing. But above all else, the most important proof is the recognition of our clients, our suppliers, our financial backers and our accountants. Once we reach this particular objective, our business activity will receive the support of our entire entourage. With the support that comes with the recognition of success, the survival and growth of our business is almost certain.

What I am referring to is the synergy of consensus. If most people we do business with are convinced that our activities are winning activities, they will be. Through actions and words, anyone who wishes to succeed must have the ability to create or achieve the synergy of consensus.

The Achilles' Heel of Companies

Small businesses are burdened and often threatened by the lack of working capital. I define "working capital" as the liquid resources (reserves or access to a credit line) that makes it possible for us to pay current accounts and continue developing our business activities. Unfortunately, working capital does not appear by magic, it has to be built. Generally, it comes from three sources: money invested by the company's shareholders or owners, credit made available by a banking institution and surplus money generated by production, in the form of profits.

If a company lacks working capital or if it manages working capital inefficiently, it is doomed to a premature death or to chronic underdevelopment. The availability and sound management of working capital enables business to move forward to maintain good relationships with its suppliers and to continue with the development of new products.

Banks

To succeed, I must build my credit rating. Borrowing and repaying on time is the most efficient way of building my credit rating. When I set up a business, banks usually are unwilling to give me credit and they do so only in exchange for personal guarantees. When my credit rating is well established, I can capitalize on my relationship with the bank by negotiating a line of credit for current operations or I can secure financing to achieve my long-term expansion goals.

Banks seek to make loans involving the least risk of default. To build a good relationship with my bank, I must be in a position to borrow only as much as I know I can repay.

The Art of Public Relations

People often underestimate the value of public relations. In my view, public relations play a very important part in any project. Public relations involves creating an image, selling ideas and concepts, building and maintaining ties of communication. Individuals who want to succeed must develop skills in the art of public relations because they seek the support and cooperation of others. No one can rely on power or constraint to force people to cooperate. The best option is using conviviality to create a positive influence over others.

Today, I understand the importance of public relations, not only when I do business with my clients and suppliers, but when I want to get results from the members of my team. Anger, threats and constraints serve no purpose. By using gentler and more positive methods, I can succeed in creating allies and in achieving my target goals.

Setting Aside the Material World

At times we may feel or we may be certain that to succeed, we must be in harmony with the material world. If we want to make money, we must live and work in the real world. If we want to experience material success, we must play the game and become materialistic. But the truth lies elsewhere. I believe that to succeed, we must set aside the material world. Our priorities must be our dreams, our ideas and our intentions. When we fall into the trap of the material reality around us and when we forget that first and foremost we are spiritual beings, we lose the urge to seek success.

Today, I am fully aware that I live in a material world, but my priorities are my ideas, my dreams and my intentions. From my ideas comes the spark of creativity. From my dreams comes the ability to create and build a glorious future. From my intentions comes the fire that pushes me to take action and to improve my life.

Creating an Objective Structure

I have a vision. I see a business that runs smoothly, with a fine, highly motivated and competent work team dedicated to developing quality products. I see a business that generates major profits, that is active on all domestic markets and that exports to several countries around the world. I dream of a company that is run efficiently and that rewards its employees generously. I see a company that is admired and respected by its competition. I dream of a company that is independent, that will carry on and continue to grow when I am gone.

Today, I see how important it is to build a company that will become an objective structure. Eventually, I will be able to leave the company, knowing that I have built a structure that depends not on any one person, but on the concerted efforts of a dedicated and committed team.

Reflections on Prosperity

Prosperity is closely linked to affluence or abundance. In other words, it is an extraordinary surplus. We can easily see that only a minority of individuals on this planet experience true prosperity. So why is it that while most of us can barely earn or produce enough to meet our own needs, others spend and consume extravagantly? Some of us are destined to fight to eat each day, while others attract the greatest riches in the world!

We could think that part of the answer lies in intelligence, talent, cunning or luck. But these factors are only part of the answer. At the core of the question of prosperity lies another, much more important factor, but one that is hidden and can't be seen by the naked eye. People who achieve prosperity have the ability to "have". They can have more. Others can have just enough or they can't have anything at all.

Bartering

Today, I see that trading products and services, bartering, can play an important part in my success. Bartering lets me trade my product for another useful product without using money. Small entrepreneurs have understood the value of bartering in the day-to-day operation of their businesses. Of course, in our society it is impossible to live solely by bartering, but its judicious use can reduce our operating costs, increase our sales and reduce our dependence on monetary transactions.

There are more and more business groups set up to encourage bartering among their members. When a business is small, bartering can be a way to establishing lasting ties. Today, I do more than sell my services for money. I trade my products and services. By doing so, I use all the avenues open to me to develop my business activities.

Gifts and Symbolic Exchange

Gifts have always played a very important part in our societies. Anthropologists who have studied donations have seen that we give gifts to particular individuals for specific reasons. Gifts are part of a symbolic exchange. I give a gift in the hope of creating or nurturing a certain degree of reciprocity. I do not give gifts haphazardly, but with the conviction that I will receive something in exchange. There is a type of equilibrium in that symbolic exchange, even if it cannot always be clearly understood. By giving, we put the other person in our debt. Sooner or later, he or she will try to repay the debt to restore the equilibrium in the relationship. Of course, in our societies of overconsumption and reward for negative productivity, the symbolic power of gifts has diminished significantly. However, gifts remain an excellent way of encouraging reciprocity.

Creating Loyalty

Today, I see how important it is to create loyalty among my key employees and my main business associates. The notion of loyalty is based on the principle that each person seeks to satisfy his or her own interests. If I want to attract and keep competent individuals on my team, I must offer them interesting advantages. Companies offer bonuses and other advantages, set up profit-sharing programs and issue shares to ensure that their workforce is stable. In this way, employees are more likely to give maximum effort and to lose interest in seeking employment with the competition.

Today, I agree that I must set up a system to reward the members of my team. I want to give them an incentive to show their commitment to the company and so I must find a way to encourage excellence and a sense of belonging.

Why Succeed?

I have asked myself the question: Why succeed? Why not let life's circumstances determine what happens to me? We often hear that we should let go and refuse to fight against the dynamics inherent in life and its events. So why not let go and let fate take care of things? For me, succeeding means becoming increasingly aware that I am the master of my own destiny, becoming increasingly capable of shaping the circumstances in my life, becoming increasingly able to be myself, someone who is conscious of my choices, my actions and my responsibilities. The world belongs to those who agree that they shape their own fate, those who agree to act and to create effects.

Today, I seek to succeed because I am powered by a profound desire to determine my own fate. I want to create and communicate. I want to grow and to extend my sphere of influence. I want to enjoy positive and nurturing experiences. I want to love and I want to experience my life and my relationships with a passion that is unique to me.

Reading Between the Lines

I pay attention to underlying messages. Not many people are skilled at the art of authentic communication. So they have to rely on more indirect forms of communication and at times, more deceitful forms. Of course, there are nonverbal messages. But there are also underlying messages that can go unnoticed if I am not attentive. So I pay close attention and I try to read between the lines. By asking the right questions, I am in a position to understand the other person and the situation more clearly.

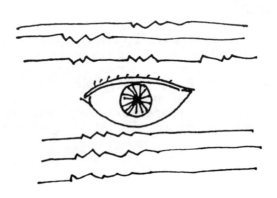

What is My Destiny?

I sometimes believed that I was destined to accomplish great things. I was born under a lucky star. I believed that as I grew, my presence would have a real impact on life and the world in general. I believed that I was destined to succeed. Time and events have made me understand that greatness is reserved for those who can reach beyond the fight for existence by creating something new, something great, something wonderfully unique. The challenges reserved for those who wish to accomplish great things and bring about great changes are enormous. The work and dedication involved is beyond imagination.

Today, I am satisfied to see that I do good things and that I am the master of my own destiny. By working conscientiously each day, I take my place in this world and I accomplish good things. Perhaps I am destined to do great things. But today, I am content with doing the right thing.

255

Assuming My Responsibilities

Finally, I have understood and admitted that I have my share of responsibility for everything that happens to me. I cannot put the blame entirely on others. Instead, now I tend to ask myself the question: What did I do, or not do, to make this happen? This leads me to be indulgent with others and to try to understand before judging them. If I fail to get the results I want, I ask myself: In light of what I did, or did not do, what explains the fact that I did not get the results I wanted? When the situation fails to unfold as I expected it to, I ask myself: What can I do to correct the situation?

Today, I accept responsibility for what happens to me. In every situation, I can see the opportunity to take action or not to take action. I can see that I have a burden of responsibility in each situation that occurs in my life.

Having Our Worth Authenticated

"We hear so much about the value of modesty and self-effacement that we feel uncomfortable when the time comes to accept that our personal worth can be authenticated and confirmed by others."
— SUE PATTON THOELE

Despite all my mistakes, despite all the improvement I could make, despite all of my imperfections, I am a being of great worth. I know who I am deep inside. I am a loving and generous person who wants to do good things. I have many wonderful qualities that I apply in day-to-day life. The people around me can easily see that I am likeable and helpful.

Today, I celebrate my qualities and my worth.

The World Has Changed

People often say that the world has changed and that old concepts have no more place in our lives. But I am not convinced that we should forget what our parents and grandparents have taught us. They included in their personal values something very important, something we tend to underestimate: dignity. In spite of the situation, we should always keep our dignity. Keeping our dignity means living with our heads held high and with a profound sense of respect and pride in ourselves. Pride dictates an attitude and behaviors based on justice and nobleness.

Today, I keep my dignity under all circumstances. I speak to people respectfully and I demand the same respect in return. I will not compromise my dignity for financial considerations or to win a battle. I see that dignity is an important part of the respect and admiration I have for myself and I want to be able to look at myself in the mirror knowing that I have been faithful to my principles.

The Power of Intelligence

None of us should underestimate the power of intelligence. We should also realize that intelligence takes many different forms. When I refer to intelligence, I am not necessarily referring to the intellect or to the size of one's brain. Rather, I am referring to conscious ability. In my view, an individual can have a very high IQ and not be able to use it. Intelligence is finding viable solutions to everyday problems, it is organizing my work and my life; it is taking care of myself and my loved ones; it is maximizing my potential and succeeding in life.

Today, I use all of my knowledge and all of my intelligence to be the person I want to be and to accomplish all the things I have promised to do. I use my intelligence to find solutions to the problems I encounter and to build a life filled with success and happiness. I use my intelligence to serve my family and my community.

Criminal Activity

In spite of what some people may think, criminal activity does not pay. Stealing, drug dealing, fraud, organized crime and all other forms of criminal activity contribute nothing to human well-being and dignity. Criminal activity impoverishes a society and those who participate in it. Our tolerance towards criminal activity leads to high social and economic costs. We all have a part to play to discourage criminal activity, no matter how modest. We also have a part to play in creating a society that can ensure that everyone has the opportunity of earning an honest living.

Succeeding Simply

The ideology of science and technology has served to create a mystery of the world we live in. People often feel left behind by the new realities of the work world and as a result, they lose hope in their ability to contribute to the society they live in. But the truth is that there will always be a place for men and women who are willing to work and who can fill human needs efficiently. Basic human needs never change. We need to eat, we need clothing, we need shelter, etc. Humans look for entertainment and they seek a social status. They need to interact with others, they often want to start a family. They need to travel to have access to all of the good things that society offers them. They also want to discover new things and grow professionally, emotionally and spiritually.

Today, I know that I can take my place in society by fulfilling a useful function which meets a human need. The range of products and services that I can offer is amazing: from housecleaning to developing specialized computer software. By taking a good look at the sector of activity I am interested in, I can set up an enterprise that meets needs and that makes people happy.

After I'm Gone

What will they say about me after I'm gone?
Will they say I was someone who loved life,
Or will they say I was just an ordinary man?

What will they say about me after I'm gone?
That I was ready to overcome all obstacles,
Or that I did what I could?

What will they say about me after I'm gone?
That I was a man of action,
Or that I always had my head in the clouds?

What will they say about me after I'm gone?
That I lived life fully, every minute of the day,
Or that they barely remember what I was really
like?

The Money We Can't Keep

I have realized that there are two types of money: the money we can keep and the money that disappears as soon as we get it. The money we can keep and spend as we choose comes to us when we have worked hard and done the best we could. It is the money we earn every day by doing a good job and by being present and active. The other type of money can come from various sources, but it involves no effort on our part. It is easy money that comes from speculation, gambling, crime, cheating or haphazard events. We can't hold on to the second type of money because it isn't really ours. So it evaporates as quickly as it came. It simply disappears.

I Express My Needs

To succeed, a relationship must allow each party to express themselves and to fulfill their needs. A relationship cannot survive if it is based on suppressing one party's needs. My responsibility is to express my own needs and to allow the other party to reach fulfillment within our relationship.

I Contribute and Let Others Contribute

I realize that there has to be an equilibrium in the sharing that takes place in a relationship. When one of the two parties contributes more than the other, it will be very hard for the relationship to survive. In addition to giving, I must be prepared to receive. I have become extremely aware of the question of sharing within my relationships because I know that inequalities inevitably lead to disappointment and failure. I cannot buy respect and love from others. Instead, I must insist on equal sharing from both sides of any relationship.

Demanding Respect

Respect is an essential ingredient in friendship, in love relationships and in work relationships. Of course, I must respect the choices, personalities and aspirations of others. But I must also insist that they respect me. Many people are so preoccupied with their need for love and approval that they are afraid of asserting themselves. I can be loved and respected. I can show other people how to respect me. I have come to the conclusion that a person who does not respect me is not worthy of a relationship with me.

The Breakfast of Champions

Today, I focus my attention on my eating habits. I realize that to succeed, I must eat properly. I must eat good things by making the right food combinations and by taking vitamins every day to stay fit and to have the energy to be productive. If my energy level drops, I will be unable to provide a consistent effort throughout the day. In the morning, I eat a breakfast that features a source of protein so that I can start off the day on the right foot.

Today, I realize that good nutrition is part of success.

School and Success

My parents taught me that to succeed later in life, I had to stay in school. They felt that quality jobs would be open only to people with diplomas. So until I was 24, I stayed in school and I earned a Master's degree. On the other hand, a prestigious job was not my reason for staying in school. I stayed in school because I liked what I was studying and I liked university life. During my years as a student, I enjoyed many wonderful experiences and I made friendships that have lasted a lifetime. I can say that I stayed in school not to succeed later on, although my education did help me. Personal interest and a love of knowledge were my reasons for staying in school.

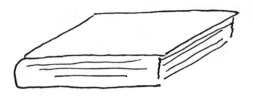

Intuition and Reason

"A man of action is more efficient if he is both emotional and cerebral — for he possesses equal parts of intuition and reason."
— FRANÇOIS GARAGNON

Success certainly requires the ability to weigh the pros and the cons, to calculate risks in relation to advantages and the reasoning that leads to the development of effective strategies. Success also requires another form of intelligence: intuition. Intuition stems from an inner source and is expressed by a sudden feeling or realization. Without the factor of intuition, success is impossible. Success is the result of creative intuition.

Today, I see how intuition plays a crucial role in my success. I must give free rein to my intuition to open new avenues. After listening to my intuition, I must use my reason to guide me and to give shape to what began as an impulse.

Material Success

Some people say that material success doesn't bring happiness or self-love. They say that nobleness and independence stem from suffering and hardship. But I have made the conscious decision of eating well, of sleeping in a comfortable bed and of travelling to see the world. I believe in material success and in all the good things that money can bring me. I also know that I could lose everything tomorrow and if I did, I would be happy to start all over again. I enjoy the game of life. I enjoy travelling on life's road as much as I enjoy arriving at its destinations. I like to succeed on every level and in every area. Why shouldn't I?

Today, I see that material success is good and noble. I give myself permission to succeed and I give myself permission to enjoy the benefits of my accomplishments. I know that material success does not make me a bad or stupid person. I am interested in life, in others and in success.

Worrying About the Future

More and more people are beginning to wonder about the future. They worry about how they will earn a living in the new global context. Jobs are changing. Technology is changing. The State's involvement in the lives of citizens is being rethought in detail. Companies are changing as well and are no longer able to create new and lasting jobs. In this new economy, we wonder how we will maintain — much less improve — our current lifestyle and plan for retirement.

Personal success calls for the ability to adapt. We must find ways to adapt to the new contexts currently emerging throughout the world and to capitalize on them. If I keep the same ideas I've always had with regard to the future, I run the risk of being disappointed. If I stay open-minded to various possibilities, I will always have the ability to adapt to changes. Each new situation brings with it the possibility of success or failure. Each context brings with it new opportunities.

Marriage

I realize that marriage is the commitment of a lifetime, but not one that should be made at all costs. I used to believe that when it came to marriage, fate had things all planned out for me. I thought that once I met the right person, things would happen on their own. But life taught me another lesson. Marriage is something built by two people, every single day. Both must take on their share of responsibilities and do their share of the work involved.

There is an important factor that determines the value and quality of a marriage: honesty. A marriage is doomed to failure when one of the partners (or both) holds back or fails to share openly. Secrets, lies and infidelity have no place in a marriage.

Today, I resolve to live in an honest and transparent manner.

Business Partners

Like a love relationship, a business partnership involves a large number of responsibilities. If I want to establish a lasting relationship, I must do my share in the process and make every possible effort to make it a success. I must communicate and consult before taking action. I must be receptive to my partner's ideas and advice. I must know how to negotiate and decide jointly. Business partnerships involve a number of difficulties, but a number of rewards come from the sharing of work and responsibilities.

Tenderness

Does tenderness have its place in the business world? We all know that love relationships in the workplace can lead to resentment and conflict. I believe that tenderness, in the form of encouragement, attentiveness, recognition and compliments, can play a very important part in good relationships between colleagues. Of course, we must be keenly aware of the limits and unwritten rules that apply to behavior between men and women in the workplace and we must be careful not to offend. But a hand on a shoulder to convey our appreciation and our encouragement, a smile to express thanks, a warm hello that means *"You're great"* — all have a definite place in the work context. Each person needs to know that he or she is liked and appreciated. Each person needs to know that he or she has a place within the organization.

Fitness and Success

Today, I take the time to keep fit. I have realized that fitness has an effect on my mental attitude and on my level of energy throughout the day. When I am fit, I am more alert and calm. I am in a better position to concentrate on my work and I feel generally better. So I take the time to exercise three or four times a week. I do exercises that strengthen my cardiovascular system and that help me keep slim. I know that fitness will give me energy and help me reach the goals I've set.

Self-Respect

Much has be written about the value of self-esteem in the past few years. We've come to believe that happiness and success are impossible without a healthy dose of self-love. But very little as been said about self-respect. I believe that the basis of success and hapiness is to be found in respecting one's self. Self-respect is not a complex psychological phenomena. It is simply behaving with diginity and grace under all circumstances. When we keep our promises, work honestly everyday, treat others with kindness and respect and strive to develop our talents and abilities, we our fostering self-respect. Without self-respect there can be no success and no happiness

Two Souls

"A relationship is based on movement, on growth; it is a sacred interpersonal environment that affects the evolution of two souls. The changes the relationship undergoes as an entity are the sum of all the changes undergone by the people in the relationship. What we ask of our relationships reflects what our relationships ask of us and of what we will become, over time."
— DAPHNE ROSE KINGMA

I have realized that a relationship is a contract. It is the union of two complete and independent people. We must define the parameters of our relationship, our conditions for satisfaction, the rules of the game. Together, we can create a common ground that goes beyond our individual ground. If I change, the changes I undergo will affect my relationship and will have an impact on my partner's life. If my partner changes, my life will be affected by those changes, because of our intimacy. I must respect the individuality of my partner and I must ask, that in return, my individuality be respected.

Today, I agree to share my growth with another person.

Delivering the Merchandise

I know that to succeed, I have to deliver the merchandise. Delivering the merchandise means consistently supplying what the client has requested. People who have the unfortunate impression that they can supply a product or a service that does not correspond exactly to the customer's expectations will soon find themselves out of work. I believe that this principle applies in all sectors of activity and in all areas of business. Consumers, employers, the public and tax payers are increasingly demanding. They want quality work, responsible and justifiable use of resources and products that meet their expectations.

Today, I know that I must supply prime quality work if I want to succeed. My success depends directly on my efforts and not on exterior factors. If I strive to offer a prime quality product, I will never be out of work.

Putting an End to Indecision

Today, I see how indecision can reduce my chances for success. I must be able to make decisions every day and to live with my decisions. Before deciding, I do my research. I question and I analyze various alternatives. I have placed myself in a situation where I must make important decisions on my future and the future of the people who work with me. By consulting my colleagues and by considering the pros and cons, I can decide. If I happen to be wrong at times, I can take responsibility for the consequences of my decisions.

Today, I resolve to make decisions and to continue along the road that leads to my goals. I know that if I am indecisive, I can miss out on good opportunities and I can hinder my own development. I can make decisions because I trust myself and I can live with the consequences of my choices.

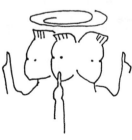

How to Mend a Broken Heart?

Most people have experienced a breakup at least once in their life. A failed relationship can have a very profound effect on us. We can stay focused on the pain for months, even years. And finally, when our heart begins to heal, we love fearfully, afraid to live through the same intense pain once again. We realize that a breakup is very similar to the experience of losing a close relative. A breakup brings out feelings of failure, abandonment, mourning, anger and denial that can be overwhelming. The pain is worse when we have been rejected by the other person in the relationship and the resulting loss of self-esteem makes our emotions even stronger.

The only cure for a broken heart is to grow, to move on, to look straight ahead and to move forward. We must seek to overcome our pain and loss. We must give up our illusions on relationships and realize that everything changes and no one can bring us happiness. We must go out in search of our own version of happiness, and no one else's.

Location, Location, Location

When I was young, a businessman taught me that there are three important factor in the success of a business: 1) location; 2) location; 3) location. Of course, he was referring to the main factor that contributes to the success of a retail business. When a retail business is well located, it easily attracts a clientele. Customers look for convenience and easy and quick access. If your business is located on a main thoroughfare, in a nice location, you are all the more likely to attract a clientele.

So it's simple: if I want to set up a retail business, I have to choose a good location. I need to analyze different locations and then I need to choose the best one, depending on where my target clientele is. Can people come to the location on foot? Is it located near parking space? It the location visible and easy to reach? Today, I see how important the question of location is.

The Gift of Friendship

I rejoice at the friendships I've made along the way. I salute myself for choosing the right friends and I forgive myself for placing my trust and my respect in certain individuals who failed to appreciate my gift of friendship. Now I can share my friendship wisely. I also see that success includes a rich and diversified social life. I seek to develop warm friendships based on affinity and the sharing of interests. I surround myself with friends who value me and who want to encourage me on my road to success.

Ending a Negative Relationship

Business relationships should be based on integrity, communication and the reciprocal interests of each party. I have realized that I can't do business with people if I can't trust them. When I feel let down, I do a little investigation. I seek to determine if my feeling is justified or not. Most situations and most problems can be resolved with frank and open dialogue. However, if the situation that is worrying me persists despite reassuring words, I must react.

We may believe that if we end a negative business relationship we may suffer a drop in revenue and a financial loss. In the short term, this may be true. But in the long run, we will emerge the winner since we will have eliminated a problem and brought order to our business activities.

Simplicity

"All we need to feel happy can be found here and now — all we need is a simple heart."
— NIKOS KAZANTZAKIS

Without denying the importance of past events that may have been painful and traumatic, I do not think that we are inevitably chained to the demons of our past. Believing that we are would amount to saying that I am a puppet, incapable of controlling my own destiny. When I manage my business soundly and when I apply authentic values such as honesty, respect and loyalty in my day-to-day dealings, life is much less complicated and much easier. Life is filled with obstacles and at times we feel the burden of past failures. But if I show determination and if I remain faithful to my principles, I run much less risk of falling into depression and anxiety. If I keep an open mind and if I seek to resolve conflicts, if I rid my life of all annoyances, if I refuse to keep a grudge or to seek revenge, I will keep a light heart and a mind that is open to positive experiences.

Hard Days

Some days are harder than others. There are days when nothing seems to go right and everything seems to go wrong. There are days when doing even the simplest things seems like a major challenge, perhaps even an exploit. On days like these, we wish we'd stayed in bed.

But overall, things usually go quite well. Overall, I feel quite satisfied. Overall, I believe that I'll manage in the end. Overall, I'm happy to be here, I'm happy to be alive, even during harder times. I don't live in hope. I live with the certainty that tomorrow will be a better day.

Today, I'll do my best and I'll get through. Today, I'll try to keep a sense of humor, even when everyone around me seems to have lost theirs. Today, when the day is over, I'll take a nice, warm bath by candlelight and I'll think of all the beautiful tomorrows awaiting me.

The Quality of My Relationships

I have realized that the quality of my life is largely determined by the quality of my relationships.
I can evaluate the quality of my relationships by
the level of communication, the balance in sharing, the respect and the affection they involve. I
must be sure that the people who share my life
are honest and that they sincerely want to contribute to my well-being. This is fundamental.
When I see that a relationship — be it emotional
or professional — does not contribute to my well-
being, I must act quickly to fix it or to end it.

Promotion

Promoting a business — and the products or services it makes available — plays an important part in its development. Promotion can take various forms: paid advertising, promotional articles, media campaigns, promotional campaigns, contact with retailers, product placement, etc. All these promotional efforts have the objective of making the product known and inciting the client to buy it. The more visible and attractive a product is and the more carefully geared it is to the expectations of clients, distributors and retailers, the likelier it is to sell well.

Small businesses must carve out a place in the market by ensuring that their product is well known and well accepted. Promotion must be ongoing and well planned to generate interesting results. To create a real impact, promotion should be carried out on several fronts, using several different methods. Businesses should also be aware of the costs involved in advertising and promotion and should find methods that provide the best results at a predetermined cost.

Long-Term Relationships

Today, I cultivate and strengthen my long-term relationships. I take a few minutes to write a letter or to make a phone call to the dear friends that play an important role in my life. I know that my most important relationships are those that have stood the test of time. These friends have accompanied me on my path in life and they deserve to hear from me. They will be very happy to know that I'm thinking of them and our contact will serve to revitalize our deep affection for each other.

Today, I celebrate long-term relationships that remind me of who I really am and where I come from.

Added Value

The value of a finished product lies in its added value. Added value is generated by the work needed to transform raw materials or semi-finished products into usable objects or products ready for sale. I am in the added value business. With my work and by coordinating the work done by others, I succeed in manufacturing goods that can then be used and consumed. My product's added value, the work that goes into it, gives it its ultimate value.

The Stock Market

I spent years playing the Stock Market. Each day, I bought a newspaper and looked through the Stock Market quotes to see if the trend was good or bad. Each day, I researched how specific securities, options and contracts were being traded. And at the end of each year, I calculated what my transactions had brought in and very often I was disappointed to see that I had made very little money in the end. The only people who make money on the Stock Market are those who put their money into good securities and then forget about the investment. After a number of years, they realize that their investment has risen in value.

The Stock Market is filled with speculators, gamblers and profit-seekers. They live off the Stock Market. And they greet you with open arms and then rob you blind. You have to be someone exceptional to beat them at their own game. Those who invest in solid, long-term stocks have the best chance of making money on the Stock Market.

Between Heaven and Earth

Today, I am somewhere between heaven and earth. I see that my ideas and my intentions will eventually take on a material form. This will happen because I say it will happen. And I say it with conviction, because I have the capacity to make my dreams come true. Today, I live between the clouds and the deep blue sea. I see that the future promises good things for me because I am a person of action, who dares to dream and who gives form to the ideas in my imagination. Today, I live between the sun and the mountains and I see that my decisions are filled with strength and energy. Today, I live between the moon and the rivers. My intentions and my ideas are undergoing constant transformation and I can transform them into realities.

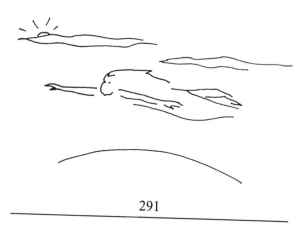

Asking for Forgiveness

"Denying responsibility when you've harmed someone can only reinforce your sense of guilt. The best way to find freedom is to admit to the error of your ways, to ask for forgiveness and to repair any damage caused."
— SHARON WEGSCHEIDER-CRUSE

I am a wonderful person and a human being. By making this statement, I recognize that I am undergoing a process of discovery and learning and I realize that I can make mistakes. By taking responsibility for my mistakes and, if necessary, by asking forgiveness for the harm I have caused, I keep my road to self-fulfillment free of obstacles and free of guilt.

Today, I see that I have the strength and conviction to recognize my mistakes and to ask for forgiveness.

Market Tests

Market tests should play an important role in the development of new products and new services. Market tests are a way to gauge the tastes, needs and expectations of customers before going ahead with the production and sale of a product. By doing market tests, I can avoid spending major amounts on a product that will not be successful. By testing the market, I can tune into my customers and I can make any necessary adjustments to my product.

Today, before investing major amounts on the development of new products and services, I do market tests. I study how customers react to my product and I evaluate its sales potential. When I listen attentively to the market, I play a winning game and I avoid costly errors.

The First Reaction

Each day, I see that my first reaction to a problem is rarely the right reaction. When something doesn't turn out as I expected it to, I tend to want to argue or use intimidation or anger to rectify the situation. But this type of reaction serves only to make matters worse. So I always take time out before reacting to this kind of situation. Depending on the circumstances, I take a few seconds, a few minutes or even a few days. The pause helps me take my distance and recover my calm. After pausing, I can see clearer and I can discuss the matter reasonably.

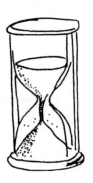

Long-Term Work

I have decided that success calls for long-term work. Of course, I experience small victories each day and I enjoy day-to-day successes, but I know that I want more. I like building. I like sowing seeds and watching them grow into trees. I like to see things come to maturity. Over the years, I've seen myself grow and I've seen myself become wiser. Over the years, I've seen myself become more aware and more serene. Over time, I truly enjoy the things that I have created and I have the common sense to nurture them and to let them grow.

Yes, I will be here tomorrow. Yes, I will be here for you, the dear friend who accompanies me on the wonderful adventure of life. We are survivors, you and I.

The Quality of Life

There should be an equilibrium between success and the quality of life. If I am always working and if I never take the time to smell the roses, how can I claim that I am on the road to success? Success means enjoying each minute and establishing an equilibrium between dedicated work and sheer pleasure. I want to live my life to the fullest and I want to experience the good things it has to offer. I want to have fun as I work and I want to laugh with my friends and my family members.

Today, I know that when life becomes too serious, painful and depressing, I am moving away from my objective of success. When I see this sign, I change course and I take my distance. I know that it is high time for me to have fun. Today, I understand that success is born of equilibrium.

Black Markets

We must work together to find solutions to the problems confronting our businesses. Some workers complain that they pay too much taxes and they look for ways to hide substantial portions of their income from the tax department. But trying to hide income leads us to act illegally. In addition, when we ask to be paid in cash, we ask our employer to act illegally. This vicious circle creates an unhealthy and negative climate that hurts economic growth and personal success.

Today, I agree to follow the rules of the game. I agree to be a full-fledged member of society and to be part of the solution, not part of the problem. I know that I will have to work even harder to achieve my financial objectives but in the end, I will feel satisfied with myself and I will have peace of mind, knowing that I've done my fair share for the greater good of all.

Silence is Golden

I have realized that in business, I must be capable
of listening more often than I talk. I must protect
my company's assets and I must be discreet,
choosing collaborators who show discretion
themselves. The company should be voluble with
regard to existing products and quiet with regard
to its internal operations, the products it has
under development and its market expansion
strategies.

Today, I listen, I look and I keep quiet. With time,
I have learned that silence is golden.

Exporting

Generally, domestic markets are offer limited avenues because they are targeted by large and aggressive foreign companies. Our lifestyles and our values are increasingly threatened by outside forces and we cannot afford to withdraw and hope for the best.

We must look at the stakes and major commercial trends in today's global marketplace. We must protect our domestic market share while also looking to the world for new opportunities.

Today, I look at the big picture and I consider the possibility of capitalizing on the opportunities of the global market. I look at export opportunities and I know that I can succeed globally as well as domestically.

The Consumer's Point of View

Consumers are no fools. They are increasingly selective. More and more, they want exactly what they're looking for, not an approximation. They quickly turn away from a product if it fails to reflect their needs. They do research, compare prices, analyze quality and act less and less through habit or impulse. Consumers are aware of the choices available to them and of the very wide range of products on today's market. They are solicited continuously and have become indifferent to the various forms of advertising and publicity. They seek to cut down on consumption and increase their quality of life. They set priorities and stick to them.

Today, surviving and prospering in business requires a great deal of effort. I have to know precisely what my customers want. I have to offer quality products that reflect my customers' expectations. And I know that my customers' demands will make me stronger and will make me a better retailer.

Small Suppliers

The vitality of the economy can be measured by the number of small suppliers who manage to do good business. I respect and admire individuals who, with fewer resources, seek to earn a living by supplying quality products and services. Small suppliers work hard to carve out a place in the market and to build a client base. I recognize the effort they make and so I pay them promptly, as soon as I receive their invoices. I seek to contribute to their survival and to their growth by giving them work and by encouraging them in their efforts to succeed.

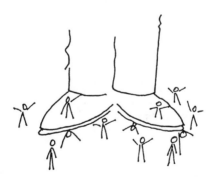

Creative Artists

We tend to underestimate the work of creative artists in the world of industry and commerce. But when we look around us, we see how important creative work is. Design, innovation, packaging, architecture and fashion are the results of the work and value added by creative artists. They give form to ideas, they fill the visual and tactile landscape with their sense of beauty and their imagination. The creative artist brings us the new and the extraordinary. The creative artist makes the world interesting and rich for each of our senses.

Today, I pay tribute to the creative artists who touch my life and who contribute to my business. Creative artists are worthy of all my respect and all my admiration.

Good Managers

Good managers know how to work with people and how to get the most out of the synergy of a team. Good managers can foresee and plan for the consequences of each decision. Good managers are diplomatic. They know how to handle difficult situations. Good managers are not afraid of confronting problems and they know how to find practical solutions. Good managers respect their commitments and their appointments. Good managers know how to count and they know how to allocate resources. Good managers are understanding, but firm. They know how to set limits. Good managers have self-discipline. They know how to make an effort to get the results they want. Good managers know how to encourage and compliment the members of their team. They also know that each team member has specific responsibilities and must contribute fairly to the overall work load and to the success of the organization.

Today, I salute and I tip my hat to all good managers. I see that the success of industry, commerce and the government depends on their efforts and their commitment to make things run smoothly.

The Civil Service

We have developed a very negative perception of what civil servants do. We imagine them taking long coffee breaks or staring out the window, while in the meantime, we're working to the point of exhaustion to earn our living. This resentment may stem from the fact that we pay income taxes without the feeling or the certainty that we are getting something in return. We see civil servants as a bunch of parasites that sap our money. This perception is totally false.

Based on my experience, civil servants work hard to earn their salaries. They are burdened with the responsibilities of an enormous bureaucracy that does very little to encourage initiative or offers little opportunity for independent thinking. The problem doesn't lie with civil servants, but with the very nature of a state bureaucracy that has become too enormous and too complex. Luckily, we are now witnessing a gradual paring down of state bureaucracies everywhere in the world.

Unions

In the past ten years, unions in America lost alot of their power. Companies had reached such a point of non-profitability and non-efficiency that they were forced to close a large number of plants and lay off hundreds of thousands of unionized employees. Meanwhile, work shifted toward countries where unions were virtually nonexistent. Today, America is experiencing a prolonged period of inflation-free prosperity. Plants are reopening and work is returning. Why? Because companies need to achieve sufficient profits to ensure their growth. They must operate in a climate that encourages development.

Organizing employees is certainly a good thing because it prevents injustice and exploitation. But in the current context of fierce international competition, employees must work with management to achieve maximum production efficiency.

I Am a Role Model

Each person is a role model. Some role models show authentic virtues such as courage, kindness, charity, competence and compassion. Because of their attitudes, their appearance and their behaviors, other role models project less positive attributes, such as laziness, greed, violence, perversion or indifference. We are social beings. We come into contact with other individuals who may be easily influenced. They look around them and they see many potential role models. They must choose their particular role model and their own modus operandi. But I can have a positive influence by being a role model that projects positive values.

Today, I understand that I am a role model for the people around me. So through my attitudes and my behaviors, I try to have a positive influence on others.

Wanting to Succeed

Today, I understand that I must want to succeed. Succeeding is an act of will, it is not a matter of luck. Succeeding isn't winning the lottery or inheriting a sum of money from a rich uncle; it is the sense of accomplishment and pride that we have when we work hard and well to achieve a goal we have set for ourselves. Succeeding is overcoming all obstacles and all disagreements around me to reach my most cherished objectives. Succeeding is fighting to keep something that I have earned through hard work. Succeeding is using my intelligence and my creativity to serve my family, my community and my country.

Today, I want to succeed because as I move forward on the road to success, I will discover who I truly am.

Children and Work

Children love to work. They particularly like to work with their parents. It's easy to see that they want to help. At times we may feel that their efforts serve mostly to slow down the operation, but I believe that we should be patient and we should encourage them. Our children will have to find their own way in life. It is important that they discover the value of work. And they can learn this very important lesson at home.

Today, I welcome my children's help. I help them help me. I show them how to make things and I let them participate. I like seeing children getting involved and eagerly doing their share.

Recognizing True Worth

Economists often refer to the law of supply and demand. When we try to determine the price of a given item, we can see that the law of supply and demand provides an explanation. The more an item is in demand, the higher its price will be, because at a given time, demand will surpass the ability to provide the product. In other words it will surpass the supply. The rarer and more popular a product is, the higher its price can be. The law of supply and demand works the same way on the job market. When there are many job openings and few people who can fill the openings, employers must pay higher salaries to attract candidates. Today, we are faced with a situation where there are more workers for a smaller number of job openings. This has the effect of reducing the salary an employer is willing to pay since offer largely surpasses demand.

Of course, there are many other factors that influence market prices, but the law of supply and demand lets us understand the fundamental dynamics of pricing.

Protecting Your Reputation

It takes years to build a good reputation. And it can be destroyed in a few seconds. Our reputation is the image other people have of us. It takes a great deal of time and effort to build an image of trustworthiness, efficiency and reliability. A good reputation is worth its weight in gold and we must protect it and nurture it throughout our career by doing good work.

Today, I recognize the value of a good reputation and so I strive to protect it by working honestly and conscientiously. I refuse to give into spur-of-the-moment impulses and I work seriously and responsibly.

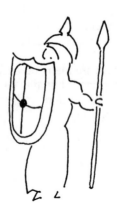

Satisfaction on the Road to Success

Today, I realize that success in not an end, it lies on the road that leads to that end. I succeed when I am happy in my day-to-day work. I succeed when I give my all and when I accomplish what I set out to do. Joy does not come at the end of the road, but along the road itself. I already feel a deep sense of satisfaction and pride when I travel the road I have chosen for myself.

Taking Full Responsibility for Problems

Problems look very different when we are willing to take full responsibility for them. The attitude that makes things move forward is the attitude of believing that there is no problem without a solution; in other words, no matter what happens, I can take care of it.

Today, I know that I am capable of solving any problem. I refuse to be intimidated by problems. On the contrary, I will use them to become stronger. Today, I see that there are no problems, only solutions.

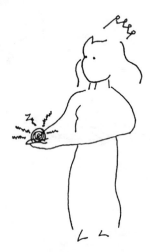

Get Your Hankerchiefs Ready

"Feelings live within us like a river and flow through our consciousness like an endless current. They travel through fear, sadness, shame and anger to be transformed into joy, delight, exuberance, excitement. At any time, we can touch and discover what we are feeling. By affirming our feelings, we transform them into an audible language and we discover a way to express the emotions that are the undercurrent of each of our lives."

— DAPHNE ROSE KINGMA

Like waves on a beach, feelings come, and then they go. I do not cling to one feeling in particular; instead, I let come and then let go. Sometimes I feel sad, melancholic or angry. These feelings emerge suddenly and I let them come and then go without any great concern. And when they go, calmness returns. I have learned not to resist feelings. I embrace them. I welcome them.

People Who Support My Success

Today, I pay tribute to all the people who support my success. I pay tribute to my family, which is there to love me and encourage me. I pay tribute to the mailman who delivers letters and packages to my office each morning. I pay tribute to the people who remove snow from the streets so that I can get to work safe and sound. I thank the members of the team that works with me every day. I pay tribute to the customers who buy my product and who contribute to my company's growth. I warmly congratulate all the people, big and small, who have no objection to my success and who are there to lend a helping hand when I need one.

The Far-Off City

Behold the gentle light of dawn
Bringing with it a message
Of hope and joy

Behold the morning shyly showing
Its beautiful and benevolent face
Behold the peaceful light
Shining on the foggy mountaintops

Behold the world
As I open my eyes on a new day
And for the first time
I see the horizon and the far-off city

Behold my hands are ready
To touch, to feel, to build
This new life before me
The new life: today

Access to Credit

At times we are surprised to see the number of personal and business bankruptcies that occur each year. Our system allows those who are unable to meet their financial obligations to liquidate their assets and eliminate all debts they may have accumulated. Declaring bankruptcy may seem like a quick and painless way to get out of a bad situation and start again.

But a bankruptcy has a negative impact on all those who have cooperated with us and with the company as a whole. This kind of situation should be avoided at all costs and the best way to prevent it is through sound management of our business activities. We must prepare ourselves for unforeseen events by setting aside a reserve fund. Financial failure has a long-term effect not only on our access to credit, but more importantly, on our reputation and our future capacity to succeed.

Today, I know that to succeed I must protect my access to credit by reimbursing my debts and managing my expenditures wisely.

Celebrating Competence

Anyone who is competent attracts admiration. I never get tired of watching an experienced artisan at work. When I was younger, we used to go to an annual village event that was called "The Traditional Crafts Fair". For a whole weekend, the village and its residents travelled back in time and celebrated work well done. Artisans arrived from the four corners of the country: carpenters, weavers, potters, glass blowers, etc. They reproduced the traditional gestures that they themselves had learned from their elders. I remember that it was a feast for the eyes. The skill and mastery they demonstrated drew the admiration of onlookers.

I want my work to earn the same respect, not out of vanity, but out of pride. When I myself look at a task or an assignment that I have just completed, I want to feel the satisfaction of a job well done. And I feel responsible for every job that I undertake. While it may not always be possible to do what we like, we can always like what we do. It's a matter of honor. When I accept a job, no matter what it may involve, I make a commitment to deliver what is expected of me.

Pleasure and Security

I have realized that most people live somewhere between pleasure and security. When they are young, they opt mainly for pleasure, keeping an eye on security. As they grow older, they opt for security, keeping an eye on pleasure. They feel as if pleasure and security are external to them and could one day disappear; and if that happened, they would be left with only sadness and hunger in their lives. Yet pleasure and security exist within us!

I am not afraid to take well calculated risks because I know that I can always recover from a negative outcome. I need not worry whether my children will always have enough to eat because deep inside me, I know that no matter what happens, they will be well fed. I am not afraid of losing what I have, the world is filled with all sorts of things that are looking for an owner. Today, I live my life with a feeling of pleasure and a feeling of security.

A New Adventure

Today is the start of a new adventure. I decide to set out with the intention to create and to build. I know that I have within me all of the talents and all of the resources I need to succeed. I put the mistakes of the past behind me and I look straight ahead, towards a glorious and exciting future.

Today is a new day. A day filled with hope and possibilities. I embrace with open arms this new day and this new life that is just beginning. I have decided to work even harder and even more intelligently to achieve the objectives that I have set for myself. I have also decided to include the fundamental values of honesty, integrity and competence in my life, because I realize that I am on the road to success.

Opening Your Heart

"The person who does not reflect the image we have of someone who deserves to be loved — the homeless person in the park, the strange character who travels up and down the street on a tricycle decked out in dozens of pennants — is precisely the person who, because he doesn't fit with our preconceived ideas, forces us to broaden our field of vision and our ability to love. See if you can open your heart — not only to those you can give it to effortlessly, but to those who need it as well."

— DAPHNE ROSE KINGMA

When I look at contemporary businesses, I am sorry to see that we place very little value on kindness and willingness to help. The currents of modern thought encourage individualism. Yet even today, when I act kindly towards my friends, my colleagues or other people, I experience a feeling of well-being and joy. I would even say that I feel good only after lending a helping hand to someone.

Knowing My Rights

I have come to understand that if I want to make my way in today's world, I have to know my rights. We live in a world of rules, laws and civic responsibilities. We have responsibilities as employers, employees, heads of households, members of the community and citizens; and we also have rights. The most fundamental of rights are the right to live in peace, to earn a respectable living and to express ourselves freely. Generally, fundamental rights are respected, but we must always seek to maintain and strengthen them once they are acquired.

In an era of huge bureaucracies, large corporations and social indifference, we can easily feel that our rights are being ignored.

Today, I take the time to find out what my rights are. To succeed, I must be free to work, to earn my living and to raise my family in peace and harmony. When I know my rights, I can affirm myself and I can take my rightful place in society, without the threat of repression or violence.

Losing My Footing

When we try to move forward and progress toward a better life we can sometimes experience difficult times. We can encounter events that make us lose our footing. These sudden reversals are more frequent at the outset of an undertaking or a project, but they also occur within companies that are well established.

Faced with situations that threaten the very survival of an organization, we must adopt a calm attitude. We must pick ourselves up and take on the fight. We must not fall into the trap of feeling sorry for ourselves or passively hoping that the situation will rectify itself. We must act energetically to correct the situation, using all the resources available to us to restore equilibrium.

Today, I know that I will face difficult situations on my road to success. When such situations occur, I am ready to take them on. Rather that accepting my fate, I will look for the most effective solutions to my problems.

Achieving Self-Worth

"Anyone who is willing to work to achieve self-esteem has more than earned it and all the good things it brings."
— SHARON WEGSCHEIDER-CRUSE

I reap what I have sown with my work and my perseverance. I congratulate myself on all the fine work I've done and I take pleasure in the fact that now I am the person I want to be. I find my satisfaction not so much in accomplishments that have a material aspect, but in my heart. Now I can feel confident in my ability to do good work.

Embracing All Experiences

Today, I am open to all experiences. I am willing to embrace them all. I know that I have nothing to fear and nothing to run away from and that I can trust myself completely. I also know that the areas of life and experiences I resist will take over my life and will follow me incessantly. Today, I have stopped running and I embrace all experiences and all aspects of my life.

Now I embrace all of my feelings. I have learned that the feelings I resist take over my life and cause even more upheaval. I am capable of having feelings and of expressing them freely in the company of friends. The word "emotion" contains the word "motion". When I try to eliminate or stop the natural movement of my feelings, I imprison their energy within me. I resolve to give free rein to my emotions.

Unconditional Self-Acceptance

"Gradually, I must accept myself as I am — with no secrets, no disguises, no lies and no rejection of any facet of myself — and with no judgement, no condemnation or denigration of any fact of myself."

— ANONYMOUS

There was a time in my life when I was no longer able to live for others or to gain approval from others. There was a time when I understood that I had to accept myself and embrace myself as I was to continue growing. By accepting myself as I am, I can live in harmony. By taking myself by the hand and by welcoming myself to life, I can be happy.

I am a being of great worth. I can love myself. I can spoil and pamper myself. I can give myself permission to live, to laugh and to have fun. I can make the choices that contribute to my well-being and to my self-fulfillment. I can learn, grow and change. I deserve a life filled with love, joy and pleasure. I deserve to succeed in all aspects of my life. I am a being of great worth.

Change

"When we undergo change, our consciousness and our view of the world is transformed. We go from one reality to a different one, but we experience both at the same time. Through this type of change, we grow and transcend into a higher state of being, to higher, more powerful and more peaceful levels of our own being. At the same time as we experience greater personal power and the full potential of the choices we make, we also begin to shoulder our responsibilities so that our life can unfold as it should."
— CHARLES L. WHITFIELD

Today, I give myself all the tools and all the support I need to continue my transformation and to make it successful. Deep inside I felt that I had to move forward because I was no longer able to accept the truth or the lives others chose to live. I know that change is a process of questioning oneself but I am able to take on the challenge because it will bring me to new horizons, to happiness and to peace of mind.

Today, I accept change. I accept to become the being that I truly am. I will follow my own lead and I will achieve serenity as I work toward my lifetime goals.

Communications in Business

Each day in the business world, an unbelievable number of mistakes are made because of a lack of communication. People barely listen to what they are told. They don't read what is written in the documents sent to them. They forget to communicate important information. Many conflicts occur because of a lack of communication and the failure to pass on information. I see how important communication is in my day-to-day work and I communicate effectively and consciously.

Today, I work at improving communications. I speak and write clearly. I ask questions to determine if people have understood the message I am conveying. I repeat what has been said to me to be sure that I have understood the message properly.

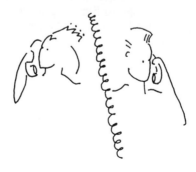

Civility

"Giving money isn't enough. Money isn't enough: money can always be found. What the poor really need from your heart is love. Spread love wherever your path takes you!"
— MOTHER TERESA

Civility is courtesy and politeness. I also belongs to a series of notions that include civilization. By definition, civilization is the opposite of barbary. Civilization is based on common rules that most people agree with and apply. Civility and civilization are closely linked. It is remarkable to see that the breakdown of society is closely linked to a breakdown in civility. It is as if our world has gone from a rigid and sometimes extreme form of discipline to an almost total indifference.

Today, I see that civility must be a part of all my relationships. I want to live a dignified and courteous life. I want to live and work in peace, so I include civility in my everyday life.

Responsibility

With time, I have come to understand that responsibility is not a burden or a test. Responsibility is my ability to accept, to receive and to have. I also see that as I accept full responsibility for myself, my actions and the things that occur in my life, I increase my self-confidence, my abilities and my control over my own life.

When I accept the fact that I am at the root of all my life experiences, I become responsible and only then can I be in full control.

Finishing Projects

"The first secret to efficiency consists in developing a deep aversion to any work that remains undone. Any work you set aside devours your energy and saps your efficiency. If you are passive when faced with undone work, you let an enemy crawl behind your lines and gain ground. In only a short while, your enemy will paralyze you completely."

— FRANÇOIS GARAGNON

The road to success and self-esteem is paved with completed projects. When I leave something undone in my life, I feel the effects. I resolve to finish all of my projects. If from the very beginning I get the feeling that I will not be able to complete a project, I just don't start it.

In the past, I didn't always finish all the projects I undertook. There was always a good reason for leaving them undone: too little time, too little money, not enough interest, etc. But now, I see that the road to success and self-esteem is paved with completed projects.

Deepening a Relationship

Long-term relationships are important in personal success. With time, we know that we can count on the other person and we know how the other person will react in a given situation. There is a relationship of trust based on experience, communication and respect. Each person's expectations are known and they are not an obstacle to negotiation. The long-term relationship is synonymous with stability.

Today, I protect and I nurture my positive relationships. I want to develop relationships that will improve and deepen with time. From a practical standpoint, a well established relationship requires less time because the work to explain ourselves and to understand each other has already been done. A long-time supplier trusts us to pay invoices on time and we know that the final product will be a quality product.

Valuing Achievement

To succeed, we must value achievement. We must value completing a project and we must value the steps involved in completing it. We must value initiating a project and seeing our initiative taking a concrete form. We should see in achievement and a job well done an expression of ourselves in the material world.

Today, I value achievement. I value what I achieve each day on the road to success. I value the days when I must go even further by going beyond my limitations and by giving my all. My work is not work — my work is my life.

Hand Made

Today, I see that when I work with my hands, I find inner harmony. By doing simple work, my life itself becomes simpler and easier. Worries disappear and I find joy and happiness. Too often, we associate success with professional work and material wealth. Today, I find much more satisfaction and a much deeper sense of achievement when I work with my hands. The inner harmony that comes with the achievement of work well done is the first form of personal success.

Never Burn Bridges

For an instant, I turned back
And I saw bridges burning behind me.

For an instant, I opened my eyes
And I saw my fallen comrades,
A sad disappointment of my doing.

For an instant, I was given awareness
And I saw that life without bridges is an island.

Today, I am a bridge builder.

Today, I am a ferry
Crossing the waves to reach you, dear friend.

Virtuous Action

In virtuous attitudes and behaviors there is a superior logic, a road that leads directly to serenity, freedom and success. But along the way, we have forgotten or lost from sight the value inherent in virtues. We have seen in goodness, kindness, compassion or gallantry something old-fashioned or outdated, no longer suited to modern life. But virtues can never be outdated because they indicate the path to salvation, divinity and success. Virtuous attitudes and behaviors are as many tangible manifestations of the true self, around which they seem to create an aura of dazzling light.

Today, I know that virtuous action holds within it the promise of success. Virtuous action holds within it the seeds to success because it opens a path from the heart to the material world of concrete achievements.

Listening

"It takes an ear of gold, an empty ear, to listen clearly."

— M.C. RICHARDS

For me, listening is a virtue. Listening means being attentive to others, being able to receive, hear and understand the communication of others. Being open to communication is the basis of any form of cooperation or relationship. So today, I resolve to develop my listening power. I am attentive to the communication I receive. I am receptive and I create avenues that others can use to communicate with me. In this way, I can break out of isolation and share my life.

Stress

As we try to find our way on the road to success, we may experience times of particularly acute stress. Financial problems, deadlines, production or management errors, personal conflicts or conflicts with colleagues, economic cycles that threaten the very survival of our companies or tax audits can cause upheaval in our business operations. These are only a few examples of the stressful situations that can affect an individual. It is very hard to feel good when we are preoccupied or stressed.

In my view, there is no miracle solution to stress. On the other hand, the worst response to stress is the use of alcohol and drugs to try to lessen the anxiety that can come with stressful situations. I have found that it is more useful to try to solve the problems that cause anxiety and stress by keeping all of my wits about me and by taking care of myself. Life is filled with different situations, some more stressful than others. I must develop the ability to work with stress while still taking good care of myself.

Increasing My Knowledge

The key to my success lies in increasing my knowledge. Curiosity is the source of invention and discovery. I know that I must do my own research and find my own answers. The more I cultivate knowledge, the more I apply it to increase my performance and the quality of my work, the closer I am to self-fulfillment. I realize that an education is not limited to formal instruction in schools and universities. I must add to my knowledge every day, throughout my lifetime.

Today, I increase my knowledge. I am here to learn and to grow. I know that by learning, by cultivating my knowledge, I can achieve self-fulfillment. I no longer wait for ready-made answers from experts and gurus, I do my own research. I do my own data analysis. I search for truth in all things.

Interest

We've all heard the saying "The more you have, the more you want". I say "The more I work, the more I feel like working and the more interest I have in working". People who don't like their work are not those who work hard, they are those who take a very casual approach to work. Bureaucratization and the division of labor have left us with jobs that are sometimes very repetitive and monotonous. But since individuals find fulfillment in their work, they must look for jobs that can meet their expectations and bring them a sense of achievement.

Emotional Support

"No one can live his life solely for himself. Thousands of strings tie us to our brothers; intertwined in these strings, such as feelings of compassion, our actions are transmuted into causes and return to us as effects."
— HERMAN MELVILLE

I can accept the help and emotional support of others. I cannot reach my goals without the help and emotional support of others. It may be true that negative experiences have led me to believe that help and emotional support are signs of weakness and inevitably lead to betrayal and exploitation. In reality though, there are individuals who are worthy of my trust and whose support I am willing to accept.

I am open to the help offered to me by others, just as I am open to offering others my help and my emotional support.

Succeeding in All Areas

Success on the material and financial levels is not all. I must seek to succeed in all areas of my life. How can I truly enjoy my professional success if my emotional life is unhappy or empty. How can I enjoy my family life if I ruin my health by abusing alcohol and drugs? How can I feel proud of my accomplishments if they are based on lies and cheating?

Today, I seek to achieve equilibrium in all areas of my life. I take stock of my life and I see that some aspects need improving. So I draw up a plan of action to improve anything that concerns me. Sometimes we need to make small changes to feel good about a situation. Equilibrium does not necessarily involve total upheaval. Sometimes all it takes to establish equilibrium is a sensible and gradual approach.

Think "Win-Win"

Today, I am convinced that success calls for an approach based on the "win-win" principle. In a transaction, a relationship or a business dealing, all parties must find what they are looking for. If the situation is based on providing an unreasonable advantage to one of the parties to the detriment of others, the result will be dissatisfaction and resentment. I seek to structure all of my transactions on the "win-win" principle. Of course, it may not be possible to strike the perfect balance between expectations, but the intention to satisfying each of the parties involved eliminates a significant number of potential problems.

Today, I know that by applying the "win-win" principle, I can build viable, long-term relationships. To do so, I must be both firm and flexible: I must find the best compromise between what is essential for me and what is essential for the other parties involved in a transaction.

Being Right or Being Wrong

Most conflicts result from the fact that we think we are right and the other person is wrong, or vice versa. Each person digs his heels and refuses to give in. Success calls for a much more flexible and conscious approach. Very few people like to be told or to admit that they are wrong. It's a matter of personal pride. And no one appreciates being subjected to domination or criticism. When I am faced with this type of situation, I try to understand the other person's point of view and I don't automatically rule it out. Then in a friendly way, I try to explain my position. When those involved step back and try to be objective, most conflicts can be resolved. However, if after discussion each person feels obligated to maintain their original position, then a simple expression of respect is all that there is left to do.

Today, I strive to respect the points of view and approaches of others. I try to see things from their viewpoint and I describe mine in a non-threatening manner. If after discussion each of us is convinced that we are right, I seek to show respect for divergent points of view.

Letting the Customer Talk

Most sales people are unaware that they talk too much. It's natural to want to convince, reassure, sustain the conversation and establish friendly relationships with clients. But I have realized that I must give clients the opportunity to talk to me. I see two major advantages in letting clients talk while I listen: 1) I am in a better position to assess their needs and expectations and to propose the best product and the best solution; 2) I give out a minimum of free information on my own business activities and I avoid being replaced by the competition.

Today, I understand the importance of listening. I encourage clients to express themselves freely and this way, I show that I am listening to their needs.

Proclaiming My Financial Independence

Today, I proclaim my financial independence. For a long time, I lived with debts and a lack of money. For a long time, I wondered how I could manage to save while still meeting my needs.

Today, I proclaim my financial independence and I draw up a plan that will help me achieve a higher level of prosperity. I have stopped spending needlessly. I have consolidated my debts and I plan to refund them as quickly as possible. I have established short, medium and long-term financial goals. I have put an end to living on the threshold of poverty and today, my goal is prosperity.

Encouraging

The effect of criticism is easy to see on someone's face. When we criticize or argue with someone, they withdraw into themselves and become silent and emotional. Criticism does very little to motivate people to improve their behaviors. Criticism is often the first reaction we have when faced with something that displeases us. A first reaction is rarely the right reaction because it is neither constructive nor well thought out.

Today, I use encouragement instead of criticism. Instead of a spontaneous reaction of criticism, I take a few minutes to think of the situation. I try to understand it and I use words of encouragement to motivate the other person.

Letting Others Love You

"By asking for what you need, you reveal your fragility as a human being and you invite the person you love to share his fragility. The reaction to an expressed desire not only brings to the person who needs help the pleasure of seeing a need filled, it also brings to the person who fills the need a feeling of effectiveness as a person and a sense of being capable of giving happiness to someone else. In such moments, each of you have the opportunity of sharing your love and your humanity."

— DAPHNE ROSE KINGMA

Vulnerability hasn't always been viewed as a desirable quality. We know that when we are vulnerable, we may be hurt. By showing others our limitations and our weaknesses, we risk becoming someone else's victim. As a result, many of us have learned not to be vulnerable. There is another side to vulnerability: the ability to ask for help and love and the potential to receive both. In this sense, vulnerability is an openness and a receptiveness.

Today, I prepare my heart to give and to receive love. Today, I open the door to others.

Outside of Me

I realize that I could easily have spent my life searching for success and happiness without ever managing to find it. I could have looked in the four corners of the earth, I would never have found them. Happiness is not something that exists outside of me. Even if I meet the love of my life, make a fortune or drive a Porsche, none of these things will bring me true happiness or personal success.

Happiness is a state of mind that results from fair behavior and a noble heart. When I love myself and what I bring to life and to others, I develop a direct relationship with happiness and success.

The Power of Visualization

We often hear that Olympic athletes preparing for a competition visualize the course from start to finish line. Mentally, they see themselves running the course and arriving first at the finish line to win the race. This method of creative visualization generates better results during the actual race. The power of creative visualization is not fully understood, but it seems to have a beneficial effect on an athlete's confidence and actual abilities.

Imagination may work in the same way. I can begin to imagine the future I would like to walk into.

Celebrating Small Achievements

For some people, tying their shoelaces in the morning is an achievement. Others are happy only if they reach ultimate heights. For my part, I like to celebrate small, day-to-day achievements such as working out to keep fit or eating well; succeeding in reaching an agreement with someone after a telephone conversation; reaching my sales objectives for the week. All these small achievements bring me closer to larger goals and encourage me every step of the way on my road to success.

Today, I celebrate all my small daily achievements. In this way, I encourage myself and I take pleasure in my work.

Living Within My Means

We've all heard the expression "living within your means", which simply means not spending more than you earn. Personally, I have never been able to live within my means. In other words, I've never really liked depriving myself of anything or being forced to live within a budget. The solution I've found to this problem is constantly striving to increase my income. My objective is to earn much more than the amount I can spend. The original principle holds true only if I am able to increase my means.

Small Gestures

"Thoughtfulness, that most wonderful of products of the human heart, expresses itself most effectively in small gestures."
— MARY BOTHAM HOWITT

The word "courteous" is the oldest adjective connected to the notion of politeness. It comes to us from the Middle Ages, which marked a new lifestyle different from the lifestyle typical of the warriors of the time. Courteous was used to describe a refinement in behavior and sensibility. So it could be said that politeness and courtesy were invented to make the world a gentler, more beautiful place.

Courtesy involves very simple gestures: taking time to say hello to someone; letting someone go ahead of you when you're waiting in line; giving up you seat on the bus. You don't have to be rich to be courteous. Polite behavior knows no barriers related to age or money.

Today, I see that by being courteous, I earn the affection and the cooperation of the people around me. Courtesy is an important ingredient in my success because by being courteous, I show that I am respectful and likeable and I show that I deserve to be supported in my efforts to achieve success.

How to Get Rich

Everyone would like to have the secret to wealth. A bit like making a cake, we could mix a few ingredients together and voilà: wealth! There are a great many books touting different approaches and recipes for increasing our income — but deep inside, we know that true wealth is reserved for a very small minority. I think that this feeling is well founded, because prosperity requires not only a deep commitment, very special skills and extraordinary determination, it requires an exceptional vision. The individuals who achieve financial wealth as a result of their own efforts are driven by a great vision, a vision they have created themselves and that they nurture throughout their lifetime.

Today, I develop my ability to see. I create a vision of greater wealth. I create and fuel a vision of myself as I am building something great, something good, something respectable.

Rare Individuals

I have been fortunate to meet individuals who, through their love for me, have changed my life. These people are my friends, they are my brothers and sisters. We recognized each other, we came together. And in spite of the distance that may separate us, we are always close. Even if a period of time goes by before we see each other again, our affection and our sense of belonging to each other is always just as strong. There are few brothers and sisters of this kind in my life. I will keep them close to my heart throughout my life's journey because they remind me of who I really am and they remind me of how generous and rich life is.

Today, I thank heaven for these rare and precious individuals who have crossed the ocean of time to come to me here. I am always a little surprised when, from time to time, I meet someone I instantly get along with, someone I feel I have known for a whole lifetime.

Self-Confidence

Personal success calls for a good dose of courage and self-confidence. I believe that we can develop self-confidence even when those around us give us no support as we grow. In such situations, we must develop self-confidence by choosing a specific activity and taking the time to observe and learn. As we become more and more successful in that activity, we build our self-confidence. A gradual approach lets us strengthen our skills and eliminate our fears.

Being

"Being happy and satisfied doesn't mean doing or accomplishing something: we need to be, not do."

— SHARON WEGSCHEIDRER-CRUSE

Now I understand the difference between doing and being. I don't need to do something to be someone. Being in and of itself is enough, appropriate actions will follow naturally. I have realized that I can't buy love or loyalty. I can't allow myself to do a series of things with the sole purpose of earning appreciation or being loved. All I have to do is recognize and experience being.

The Power of Individuality

Individuality gives me a certain power. By being an individual, I am free to think my own thoughts, to see things from my own perspective, to follow my own path. I approach each situation with my own attitudes, my own values and my own abilities. Within me I have the power of creativity and the awareness of my actions. I can take position and make my own choices. I am free to make my own decisions and to pursue my own goals. The world knows only one me. And I am happy and proud to be me.

Gentleness

"I believe that humanity will not only last, it will prevail. Man is immortal, not because of all creatures he is the only one with an indefatigable voice, but because he has a soul, a spirit capable of goodness and compassion."
— WILLIAM FAULKNER

Gentleness will always be stronger and longer lasting than brute force. Just as water shows its force in the fact that it has no resistance but can still grind stone into sand, the greatest victories are won with gentleness. Gentleness lets me deal with and eliminate all resistance.

A small, smiling child, a cat's silky soft fur, a gentle spring breeze, the caress of a loved one are all images that evoke the notion of gentleness. Gentleness is to the soul what grace is to gesture. There is no room for harshness and vulgarity in my life. I embrace gentleness.

Making a Place in the World

Now I see the world around me. A world filled with life and movement. I look around me and I see the world with a certain detachment. I look around me, from a distance, so that I can be in the best position to see, to take in, to understand life and the beings living on this planet. This will help me make the best place for myself in our fascinating world.

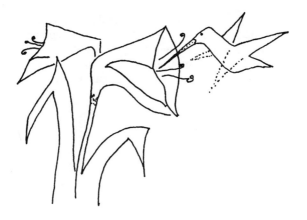

My Deeper Motives

What are the motives that drive me to succeed? Am I looking for glory, wealth, power or immortality? Do I want to succeed to avoid bearing the burden of failure? Do I want to become a responsible member of my community? I believe that the motives that drive me to succeed have an impact on my success. If they are based entirely on my own interests, it will be difficult for me to achieve my objectives. I believe that success can't be a one-way street. I can't hope to take without giving.

Today, I seek to understand the deep motives that are the reasons for my commitment to success. I know that I can find new, more valuable and more generous motives. In this way, I travel on the road to success with a soul filled with good intentions.

Producing More

To achieve greater wealth, I must produce surpluses — like as a farmer who produces food for his own consumption and a surplus to sell on the market. If I am content to produce only enough to meet my own needs, I will always be forced to work to survive. But if I produce surpluses and build reserves, I will become progressively more prosperous.

Today, I see that if I want to become more independent and more prosperous, I must produce surpluses. I must produce more than I can consume. Therefore, I work for both today and tomorrow.

Free Enterprise

Our economic system is based on the concept of free trade. This means that each person is free to trade work or products for money and others are free to buy the work or products. The fact that each individual is free to trade and benefit from trade creates a global trade system that benefits the society as a whole. Of course, many constraints and conditions exist and affect how free this trading actually is, but the principle remains viable.

Today, I am happy to be part of a system of free enterprise and free trade. I know that I can move closer to my objectives for personal success because I am free to trade and to benefit from my trading.

Our Ability to Adapt

Today, I know how adaptability and flexibility are important to my success. Each day, I am faced with new challenges and new problems that test my skills and my imagination. I see that to reach my goals, I must be capable of adapting to all kinds of situations and to all kinds of people. If I am rigid and inflexible, I will fail to capitalize on many of the situations I encounter.

By being open and flexible, I can see the positive side of things, I can change a difficult situation into a victory.

The Energy of Renewal

As the new year draws closer, I am filled with the energy of renewal and change. I am optimistic and enthusiastic as I see the new year approach. During the coming year, I will continue along my road towards my most cherished goals. I will work with the members of my family and of my work team to create a climate of harmony and joy.

Today, I feel that all is possible and that every avenue is open to me. Today, I am confident, I know that I will succeed.

Doing the Groundwork

Statistics show that the vast majority of small businesses are doomed to failure during their first years of existence. Many economists and business people have tried to determine the factors that contribute to the failure or success of small business, but knowledge of these factors doesn't seem to have improved the overall situation. I don't believe that genetic factors predispose some people to success, and others to failure. Groundwork and the knowledge of factors that contribute to the success of a small business are vital.

Success always calls for preparation work, a period during which we study possibilities and potential from a distance. During this gestation period, we can identify and accumulate the necessary resources, proceed with the necessary training, prepare mentally and emotionally to take on the challenges of the new situation, develop our new approaches and our strategies for success. Today, I agree to do the groundwork and I see that it is crucial to my success.

I've Come a Long Way

Today, I see that I have gone far. In the past year, I have come a good distance and I am proud of my achievements. I know that there are still many projects I want to realize, but I can still take pleasure in the progress I've made. Yes, I am well on my way on the road to success and I can count on myself to keep on course and to go even further. During the past year, I have found new allies and I have strengthened my commitment to excellence.

Today, I see that I have gone far in the past year.

My True Colors

Today, I let my true colors shine through. I know that I am a good, loving and generous person and I show these qualities to the people around me. I let them love me and appreciate me. Goodness, love and generosity are my main tools in life and I use them to build bridges and to succeed.

Today, I know that I am a fundamentally good person and I seek to do good things under all circumstances. To hear the voice of reason, all I need to do is listen to myself.

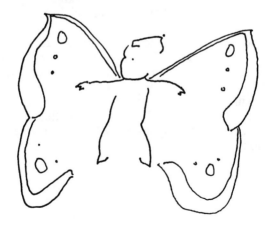

A Tribute to Small Business

The lower level of responsibility now being taken on by the State and by large corporations with regard to the well-being and survival of the individual and of families, has given rise to a new reality: the need for each individual to take charge more firmly of his or her own survival and development. This in turn results in the increasing value attached to small business. Small businesses are the purest and simplest expression of the individual or the family taking control and deciding on economic affirmation. When we set up a small business, we proclaim our independence and our commitment to taking control of our own lives and our own financial situation.

Today, I pay tribute to all those who plan to set up a small business. I see in their efforts a commitment to affirm themselves and to succeed. I understand that setting up and managing a small business requires not only a strong dose of courage, but the ability to work intelligently and to take on full responsibility for one's own situation.

Celebrating Christmas

"The Latin word agape signifies understanding and redemptive good will towards all men. It is an overflowing love that expects nothing in return. Theologians would say that it is the love of God that governs the hearts of men. When one loves in this way, one loves all men — not for themselves, but because God loves them."
— MARTIN LUTHER KING JR.

Today, I show good will toward all people. Today, I open my heart and I live in a spirit of love and forgiveness. I wish all members of my family and everyone I know a Christmas filled with love and joy. I also know that for many people, Christmas is a difficult time; my heart goes out to them and I send them my love and my kindness. Today, I am close to those I love and I share these precious moments with them.

Breathing

Today, I take the time to breathe a little. Today, I think of myself and I take the time to relax and have fun. My year has been very busy and I deserve to take a day off. Throughout this day, I will give in to the urge to do nothing in particularly and I will be content to simply be. I can sleep, eat or play with the children — this day is my very own.

Looking back

Today, I take the time to look back on this year. I review major events and I evaluate my progress. I take the time to analyze my successes and my less successful undertakings. I try to be totally detached and objective in doing this, and I draw lessons from my experiences. I try to see which actions brought me the greatest satisfaction and which led to what I consider to be my most significant successes this year.

The Results I Can Achieve

Today, I seek to clarify what I want to accomplish during the coming year. I use my imagination to create mental images of what I would like to achieve. I ask myself the following questions: What would I like to achieve in the coming year? What are the dreams I would like to see come true in the coming year? What can I do to make my life better, more enjoyable and more interesting? What can I do to achieve greater success in my work, in my family, in my relationships, in my community?

Today, I look to the future and I imagine the life that I can create. I imagine all the things that I can achieve.

Goals for the New Year?

Today, I make a list of all my goals for the new year. I look at every aspect of my life and I determine which improvements I would like to make in each one. I write down my objectives for each aspect of my life and I include a deadline for reaching them. I can make a list of objectives in the short term (one year or less) and in the long term (more than one year). Preparing a list of all of my goals lets me see them clearly. I can keep the list close, I can revise it from time to time and I can analyze my progress periodically.

My Plan of Attack

Today, I prepare a plan of attack. What are the steps I must take to reach my objectives? Concretely, what must I do to achieve my personal and professional objectives?

Today, I take out a pen and paper and I write down all the things that I will do to ensure my success. My plan of attack will include my objectives for each aspect of my life and it will also include all the actions I plan to take to achieve these objectives.

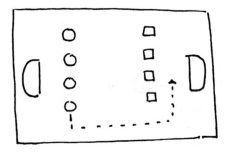

Preparing the New Year

Today, I prepare the new year which is almost here. I open my heart and I use my imagination. I look forward to all of the things I want to do and to all of my victories. I am optimistic and realistic as I prepare myself for the arrival of the new year. This year, I am ready to work hard to achieve my goals. I know that I will be confronted with certain challenges, but I also know that I can rely on myself.

Today, I am in contact with my deep commitment to succeed. I foresee all of the possibilities available to me as the new year is about to begin. I have already set my objectives and now, I prepare for success — mentally, emotionally and spiritually.

PRINTED IN CANADA